BEYOND
REALITY

D1602591

BEYOND REALITY

Augmented, Virtual, and Mixed Reality in the Library

Edited by
KENNETH J. VARNUM

CHICAGO   2019

KENNETH J. VARNUM is senior program manager at the University of Michigan Library. In this role, he is responsible for the library's discovery systems, document delivery and link resolver interfaces, and the library's evolving and emerging analytics infrastructure. Over his two decades working with public-facing technology in academic, corporate, and special libraries, he has gained a deep appreciation and understanding of the need to tailor systems and interfaces to the local user base. A frequent speaker and author, Varnum presents and writes about discovery systems, library analytics, and technology. In addition to numerous articles and chapters, he wrote *Drupal in Libraries* (2012), compiled the LITA Guide *The Top Technologies Every Librarian Needs to Know* (2014), and edited *Exploring Discovery: The Front Door to Your Library's Licensed and Digitized Content* (2016). He also edited Lorcan Dempsey's *The Network Reshapes the Library* (2014). Varnum received his master's degrees from the University of Michigan's School of Information and its Center for Russian and East European Studies, and his bachelor of arts degree from Grinnell College. You can contact him through his website at https://www.varnum.org/ or on Twitter at @varnum.

Extensive effort has gone into ensuring the reliability of the information in this book; however, the publisher makes no warranty, express or implied, with respect to the material contained herein.

ISBNs
978-0-8389-1785-5 (paper)
978-0-8389-1810-4 (PDF)
978-0-8389-1809-8 (ePub)
978-0-8389-1813-5 (Kindle)

Library of Congress Cataloging-in-Publication Data

Names: Varnum, Kenneth J., 1967– editor.
Title: Beyond reality : augmented, virtual, and mixed reality in the library / edited by Kenneth J. Varnum.
Description: Chicago : ALA Editions, An imprint of the American Library Association, 2019. | Includes index. | Includes bibliographical references and index.
Identifiers: LCCN 2018049625 | ISBN 9780838917855 (paper : alk. paper) | ISBN 9780838918098 (epub) | ISBN 9780838918104 (pdf) | ISBN 9780838918135 (kindle)
Subjects: LCSH: Virtual reality—Library applications.
Classification: LCC Z678.93.S53 B49 2019 | DDC 006.8—dc23
LC record available at https://lccn.loc.gov/2018049625

Cover design by TJ Johnson. Cover image © kiankhoon, iStock Photo.

Text design in the Chaparral, Gotham, and Bell Gothic typefaces.

⊚ This paper meets the requirements of ANSI/NISO Z39.48-1992 (Permanence of Paper).

Printed in the United States of America

23 22 21 20 19   5 4 3 2 1

Dedicated to my sister Susan,
who has probably accused me
of being beyond reality
just as many times
as I have accused her.

Contents

Preface

AT A TIME WHEN LIBRARIES ARE FACING A RANGE OF SIGNIFI-
cant challenges, including rapidly evolving needs for physical space, constant budgetary pressures, and growing concern over the confidentiality of
patron-generated data, a new technology is emerging that offers an entirely
new spin on these challenges. The suite of technologies encompassed by virtual, augmented, and mixed reality stands to open vast opportunities for new
services, expand the way library materials can be accessed and integrated into
nonlibrary venues, and alter the way we, as a society, interact with information. The real and virtual horizons these new technologies are establishing
represent a new frontier in the way we do almost everything.

What are the technologies we are describing? There are three at the
core of this book, all of them deeply intertwined with each other. We live in
actual reality—the physical world around us. By contrast, *augmented reality*
is enhanced reality, usually in a limited way. The user is perceiving the real
world, but the computer is adding objects, information, or details that are not
physically present. Heads-up displays in aircraft are an example of this technology—data such as routing information, other aircraft just past the visible
horizon, the aircraft's speed, and the like can be displayed in the pilot's field
of view without requiring a glance at the instrument panel. A possibly more
familiar example is the popular Pokémon GO game played on smartphones,
where computer-generated creatures are superimposed on a dynamic map of
where the player is actually located.

Virtual reality is the computer-created counterpart to actual reality. Through a video headset, computer programs present a visual world that can, pixel-perfectly, replicate the real world—or show a completely unreal one. With sensors in the headset to detect the direction the user is looking (up, down, left, right; rotating clockwise, etc.) and moving in a physical environment (stepping left, right, moving backward, etc.), the computer simulates the resulting changing view.

If actual reality—in which the entire area of perception is perceived, unmediated, by the human senses—is at one end of a scale, and virtual reality—in which the entire area of perception is computer-generated—is on the other, then *mixed reality* is the entire continuum between the two, spanning the range from just a bit of computer-augmented information or presentation of objects, all the way up to the near-total simulation of the world around us. In today's society, most of our routine experiences with mixed reality are toward the lower end of this scale, where we have just a bit of extra information added to our daily life by computerized technology. As a society, though, we seem to be on a path where more fully integrated virtual realities are on the near horizon, and we're moving quickly in that direction.

What do these technological advances mean for libraries? How could they shape the services we offer our users, and the ways our users prefer to interact with us? What does this overarching trend mean for instruction? And how can we be confident that our services and offerings in this area are not running afoul of intellectual property concerns? This book seeks to address these questions.

Kenneth J. Varnum
Ann Arbor, Michigan
January 2019

1

Augmented Reality

All about Holograms

IN CASE YOU HAVEN'T HEARD, HOLOGRAMS HAVE ARRIVED. THERE is an exciting new technology known as augmented reality (AR). At the highest level, AR gives us the three-dimensional holograms we see in the movies, and at the lowest level, it is a nifty technology with many practical (or just plain fun) applications to daily life. AR merges artificial digital elements with the physical world, usually by means of a headset or other digital device. As people realize its potential, it seems to grow in popularity every day. It will most likely have an impact on our lives at some point in the near future. There are many benefits of adopting the technology, but what does AR look like when implemented inside a library? In this chapter, we will look at AR through the lens of the White Plains Public Library in New York, an institution I have had the pleasure of working in for the past five years. Here, the staff have implemented AR, to the delight of many patrons. The technology is a shining example of "new." The purpose of this chapter is to inspire library professionals to explore this emerging technology and consider implementing it at their own institutions. We will discuss the various aspects and practical benefits of the technology, why libraries should adopt it, and where it is headed.

WHAT IS AUGMENTED REALITY?

The official definition of *augmented reality* is "an enhanced version of reality created by the use of technology to overlay digital information on an image of something being viewed."[1] AR essentially consists of integrating digital content with a user's visual perspective in order to perceive additional elements, thus "augmenting" a user's space. The Forbes Agency Council describes it as "the ability to integrate digital data into a real-time experience."[2] AR tricks one's brain into perceiving elements that are not physically there. Digitally added stimuli appear to exist in one's approximate physical space, but these are in fact layers of artificial content that are visually overlaid. It is a holographic illusion with promising possibilities.

AR is an exciting new technology, harboring major potential. As the technology writer Om Malik enthusiastically states, "for those who have been believers in augmented reality, these are exciting times."[3] The practical uses of AR are growing by the day. A subcategory of AR, known as mixed reality (MR), refers to the specific ability to artificially interact with overlaid digital elements. It is essentially AR you can "touch," and this ability is where some of the most exciting breakthroughs are taking place. Being able to physically interact with content that appears to be real is an incredible innovation and offers endless possibilities.

Compared to its sister technology, virtual reality (VR), AR has a greater practical application to everyday life. Instead of transporting the user to an alternate world of digital content, as VR does, AR transports digital content to the user's space, seamlessly bridging the gap between the physical and the digital world. Due to this hybrid approach, an AR user is never detached from his or her surroundings and can absorb content without being masked in an artificial, omnidirectional world, as in VR. For those of you who have tried VR, you may have discovered how disorienting it can be to put on a headset and isolate yourself. When I rode a virtual roller coaster, I was so immersed in the virtual ride that it was a good idea to have a friend standing by so I wouldn't accidentally overturn the chair I was sitting in—that's how detached from the outside world you can get inside a virtual environment. But with AR, you don't shut out the outside world. Instead, the digital content is viewed as part of your everyday life and surroundings.

In many ways, virtual reality has overshadowed augmented reality, at least in the public's eye. Millions of people are purchasing and using VR headsets, such as the Oculus Rift (www.oculus.com/rift) and HTC Vive (www.vive .com), and it has become a relatively common practice to adopt the technology in libraries and at home. AR, on the other hand, has not necessarily had the same level of success, despite being equally deserving. One of the first large-scale releases of an AR headset, known as Google Glass, took place in 2013. It gained a great deal of attention but ultimately failed as a product.[4] Thus, AR has not necessarily captured the imagination of society at the same level that VR has—yet. It may be that Google Glass was slightly ahead of its time.

But AR has been quietly integrating itself into society for years in various ways, without a great deal of public attention. Even though AR is only in its infancy (relatively speaking), it has already proven its practical applications. Whether it is an artificial line drawn on a football field, digital ads behind home plate at a baseball game, or cat ears and whiskers added to a cell phone's camera feed to achieve an interesting selfie, AR innovations have proven to be popular and useful for the general public, even if people don't necessarily understand how it is technically happening.

The evolution of AR technology shares many historical milestones with VR, such as the invention of the stereoscope by Sir Charles Wheatstone in 1838, and the first head-mounted display system in 1968,[5] but one of the first widespread, popular uses of AR technology was initiated by, of all things, the National Football League (NFL).

In 1998, a virtual "1st & Ten computer system" was developed and implemented by a company named Sportvision, Inc., to be included on a live NFL broadcast.[6] Through a technological illusion, the first-down line appears under the players on the field, as if they were physically moving over it. This yellow-colored line aided viewing of the game in real time and did so seamlessly. The first time it was used was during a game between the Baltimore Ravens and the Cincinnati Bengals.[7] It instantly gained the approval of football fans, to the point that when Fox Sports ceased providing the line in 2001 in order to cut production costs, most fans were displeased.[8] The "1st & Ten computer system" was an important step for a public becoming acquainted with AR.

Many people today are familiar with AR technology through the use of smartphones and other mobile devices and applications. Smartphones make it easy to use AR technology because they are commonly equipped with a camera, which allows for the streaming and modification of a real-time video feed, making it ripe for AR. There are several popular mobile applications that are available on major smartphones and harness this type of AR technology today, such as Pokémon Go, a game in which users can search and find virtual creatures at real-world locations; Snapchat, a communication application that includes a library of digital overlays to artificially modify a user's face; and Google Translate, a translation application that can digitally convert text from physical signs to different languages in real time.

There are several creative uses for AR technology that have proven to be worthwhile. For example, IKEA Place is an application that allows users to virtually place pieces of furniture in their room so they can observe how chosen pieces of furniture will look, augmenting what is seen through the smartphone camera's lens. The feedback of the information, in real time, creates an experience that is both helpful and awe-inspiring at the same time. It makes life more convenient, which is a great use of the technology.

It should be clear at this point that AR is becoming commonplace in society, and it may be the start of a major trend. The fact that many devices and apps now incorporate AR is an indication of a future society that will be immersed in it, and when it comes to libraries, the application of this technology is promising.

AUGMENTED LIBRARIES

There is great opportunity for libraries to integrate augmented reality. For centuries, libraries have been offering their communities the services and resources they depend on. With the relatively recent information technology revolution, many libraries have—in addition to the usual resources and services a traditional library offers—grown into educational community centers in which collaboration and learning are encouraged. As one *Chicago Tribune* contributor puts it, "in case you haven't noticed, libraries are becoming louder."[9] There is no better time to incorporate new AR technology. Accordingly, author Elizabeth Zak argues that "AR can and should be studied from every aspect of the field of LIS," but she declares this should only be done "if it is in fact a new direction toward our new normal."[10] Whether or not AR will become part of the "new normal" remains to be seen.

There have been several studies that support the use of AR in libraries. As researchers at Kansas State University propose, a library can be a more attractive place with AR.[11] They suggest it is possible to use AR as a game with puzzles to help patrons learn about library services. Another study shows that AR can enhance a patron's experience at a library, even with books. Modern pop-up books can be digitally extended, using AR technology, within the context of the work, "to rotate, tilt, and manipulate viewing angles of various objects."[12]

There are several libraries that are now implementing AR and associated technologies, and it is beneficial to observe the many ways we can now incorporate AR into existing services and also provide completely new services. For example, Diana Hellyar, a reference librarian at the University of Hartford, writes how "using apps and integrating augmented reality is a fun way to do a summer reading challenge."[13] In this particular case, they used an AR application called Mythical Maze that allows patrons "to scan stickers they receive from reading books, which unlocks augmented content via a mobile device, such as mythical creature animations."[14] Another library, the J. Willard Marriott Library at the University of Utah, offers AR and VR workshops to inspire students and faculty to use the technology within their research and areas of study.[15] (See chapter 4 for a description of these projects.) Other libraries, such as the North Carolina State University library system, lend AR and VR equipment, and they also host spaces for experiences, games, and development.[16]

Many libraries already incorporate AR in the services they provide, whether they are aware of it or not.

In 2016, many gamers were turned on to public libraries due to the Pokémon Go sensation, a popular application that uses AR technology with mobile phones. Several libraries seized the opportunity to offer a virtual "Gym," where Pokémon Go users could play the popular game in a specific location.[17] For many, this game was the first encounter with AR. Many libraries hopped on the bandwagon not only as a clever way to attract young patrons into the library, but also to encourage the use of exciting new technologies. In addition, many modern libraries are already familiar with incorporating simulation-based technologies, such as the nearly one hundred libraries in California that are adopting VR technology as part of one private company's initiative to spread awareness and distribute resources to an eager public.[18] Implementing VR, as we will see, is not far removed from implementing AR. It makes sense that AR technology should receive the same level of recognition and utilization by libraries that VR has attained, due to the former's greater immersion in the real world.

LOCAL AUGMENTATION

The popularity and capabilities of AR technology are two of the reasons why the White Plains Public Library (WPPL) became interested in it. The WPPL is an innovative library located in White Plains, New York, about twenty-five miles north of Manhattan.[19] It has been open to the public since 1899 and has been at its present location since 1974, serving a diverse population of over half a million visitors each year.[20] In an effort to educate the public and connect with a new generation of patrons, the library continually offers classes on a variety of topics, including augmented reality.

The WPPL is no stranger to innovation and is a great place for learning and engagement with new technologies. Part of the library's mission is to "offer new services that will bring adults into the library and provide them with the resources and opportunities for personal growth" and to "provide excellent opportunities for adults to learn."[21] The library has expanded its technological offerings for all ages and it now offers classes featuring AR. The recent addition of a new adult area, named "The Hub," has further expanded the library's technical offerings and spurred an interest in AR.

Back in 2013, the WPPL created a new digital media specialist staff position, to better connect patrons to the modern technological world. The digital media specialist teaches patrons to be digitally literate and provides them with the technology skills necessary for the modern world. I am the digital media specialist at the WPPL. By bringing expertise in all areas of computer-related technology and relaying that information to patrons and staff in an effective way, the library is able to provide innovative services in many technologies, including augmented reality.

Seeing the activities of other libraries, as well as observing the current technical capabilities and general "buzz" surrounding augmented reality, has led the WPPL to experiment with offering AR. With the advent of advanced AR technology, there are practical benefits to incorporating it into the library's list of resources, as we will see. The WPPL is planning to acquire an upcoming AR headset, known as the Microsoft HoloLens, set to be released in 2019, as part of its new adult area.[22] (See chapter 2 for more information about the HoloLens.) The headset would serve to expose the public to advanced AR technology and open the door to interesting new creative projects, such as AR games that can be played "on top" of any flat surface.

By preparing the White Plains Public Library to implement VR in 2017, we unintentionally paved the road to providing AR services. The library is already equipped with the Oculus Rift and HTC Vive, and it has been running VR camps, classes, tryouts, and development sessions for teen and adult patrons. With many of the legalities and logistics now in order, such as a waiver form for patrons to sign in order to use VR equipment, the library is now nicely prepared for advanced AR implementation.

Even though advanced AR headsets are not widely available, there are several ways the WPPL has already implemented AR. After acquiring VR headsets and equipment, the library began offering informative classes such as "Augmented Reality vs. Virtual Reality: What's the Difference?" in which participants took part in a discussion about the two similar, but distinct, technologies. Since AR technology is still in its infancy and not yet widely available, true implementation of it has mainly been limited to mobile applications and tablet software, such as augmented coloring-book programs.

One of the most significant ways that the WPPL has incorporated AR is through a mobile application called Quiver. With Quiver, users are able to digitally make physical coloring-book pages become fully animated, three-dimensional models.[23] Using preselected printed artwork, one fills in the colors using standard utensils, such as a crayon, and proceeds to point a tablet equipped with the Quiver app at the page and watch it "come to life." Some of the artwork takes it one step further and includes AR games that you can play "on top" of a flat surface in the physical room. At the WPPL, patrons are provided with the technology and equipment to experience this AR process. It is an opportunity to take the current coloring-book craze to the next level.

Developing and implementing the AR coloring-book class were easier to accomplish at the library than it may seem. A colleague recommended the AR coloring-book application to me, and I instantly saw the potential of the new concept for a library class. We were already equipped with a set of tablets for youth, so I knew it was feasible. It was only a matter of installing the Quiver application and testing it out. I printed out one of the designated color pages for use and then installed the application. I asked one of the teenage patrons at the library to color it in and proceeded to test out the technology. It worked seamlessly, I might add.

It required minimal effort to explain how to use this form of AR to the staff, since the process itself is intuitive. Although they were slightly intimidated by the AR technology, the staff quickly found it to be easy to use. I worked in conjunction with another staff member who ran a monthly coloring-book program for youth services, because I thought it was a perfect opportunity to test out the technology. With the Quiver application, and many other AR apps for that matter, the hardware and software take care of the complicated processing math needed to create AR, making the end process easy to use.

Having prepared the equipment and trained the relevant staff, the process of running the AR class was set to proceed swimmingly. With the application installed and preselected coloring-book pages printed, it was only a matter of showing the session participants how the process worked. The young patrons who joined the class were interested in coloring the pages and quickly filed in, ready to draw. As the teens colored, a staff member pulled out a tablet and demonstrated the AR capabilities of the coloring pages, using a particular teen's drawing as an example. This incentivized other teens who were coloring to finish so they could test out their particular page with the technology. Soon, many pre-equipped library tablets were being used to test out each teen's coloring page, and the atmosphere was playful and fun.

The response to the class was overwhelmingly positive. One of the participants, impressed by the technology, said, "It was cool how the color I put on the car you could actually see it on the car . . . you can see what you drew." He also enthusiastically stated, "I like the truck one . . . you could stop it and if you move the paper you could change the direction it goes . . . it seems futuristic." Another participant stated, "I liked the Power Ranger because it could kick and punch, and it was a cool feature." She was visibly enjoying herself using the AR technology with her artwork.

The combination of AR with a common activity such as coloring is beneficial because it attracts a variety of personalities and learning levels while at the same time making AR feel accessible. Both patrons who are interested in digital technology and patrons who are interested in creative art can simultaneously benefit from a library offering such an activity. In addition, the activity was relevant for multiple learning styles. Some patrons were happy to color and the AR features were simply an additional bonus, while others focused solely on the AR technology, testing the capabilities by drawing outside of the lines in deliberate attempts to see how the application would react.

The White Plains Public Library will likely offer more AR services in the future. It has proven beneficial to offer AR classes that harness the creative potential of smartphones and tablets to, among other things, simply allow patrons to test the technology. Although advanced AR headsets are not yet widely available, there are already plenty of related technologies for the library to experiment with in the meantime.[24] Adopting the technology will prepare the library for the future, but it remains to be seen exactly where the field of AR is headed. It is exciting to explore how patrons of all ages can use AR technology to its full potential, for both entertainment and educational purposes.

AUGMENTED FUTURE

Augmented reality has the ability to drastically change the way people live their everyday lives. Whether or not this is an improvement is a matter of opinion. Regardless, the idea that you can bring in digital information to the physical world has monumental implications. The *Forbes* contributor Blake Morgan describes how AR has the potential to revolutionize society and consumerism: "Instead of customers having to seek out information, that knowledge can now be embedded in the environment in a way that anticipates customers' needs and helps them find solutions where they already are."[25] Just imagine being able to look at a coffee shop and see how much a cup costs; look at a hotel to see what rooms are available and where they are located in the building; glance at a train station or movie theater to see the schedules; or scan items at a store by simply looking at them.

There are several potential benefits to adopting augmented reality. The technology can make life more efficient, with, for example, artificial navigation lines to help someone find his or her way in an unfamiliar building, or the ability to virtually create computer monitors and televisions without purchasing any physical hardware. There are safety benefits as well, such as a driving system created by the Swiss-based company WayRay that uses AR on a car windshield, displaying directions and hazards and more.[26] In the medical field, AR has the potential to help patients with vision-related conditions, to enable remote, patient-perspective consultations, and even to assist surgeons in the operating room.[27]

In addition, there are educational benefits of using AR. Training professionals like surgeons or pilots with AR and VR has existed for some time, but the scope of possibilities within the realm of education is expanding to include more abstract concepts for learners.[28] For example, AR can help students visualize complex processes such as respiration or electromagnetism. The educational consultant Jeremy Riel, who supports the use of educational AR technology, asks, "What if the physical space of the classroom could be used to bring digitally created elements to a student's experience?"[29] There is no telling what the educational and societal applications of AR technology might eventually be.

Based on business trends, it appears that our society is heading towards digital augmentation in a significant way. There are predictions that AR will thrive financially, with annual spending doubling in 2018 and beyond.[30] Notable companies are hopping on board with AR technology as well, such as the online retailer giant Amazon.com, which recently released tools for artificial world creation.[31] Apple Inc. recently acquired Vrvana, an AR headset startup company, for thirty million dollars, which might be an indication that the company is headed towards AR.[32] Apple has officially released the ARKit, an AR development platform for iOS devices (developer.apple.com/arkit). Even Google's parent company is attempting to bring the Google Glass headset back, apparently seeing more potential this time around in a different approach; the company is making the headset more lightweight and is giving it a longer battery life.[33] Based on the current trends, AR may be on the verge of growing exponentially in our world.

AR is generating success for regular companies, and it may be able to do so for libraries, too. The Forbes Agency Council discusses how AR can be a great asset for businesses, as with the aforementioned IKEA Place application.[34] In the same way, AR can be advantageous for libraries. Holographic technology is gaining popularity, and public libraries can serve as the bridge for the public to access this incredible new tool that is currently just out of reach.

AR technology will offer library patrons a wealth of possibilities in the future. There could be hologram conference rooms, where libraries purchase the expensive equipment for the public to experience augmented telecommunication sessions. There are also possibilities for libraries to provide resources on local and global history, such as having digital overlays of historic places, and capturing three-dimensional footage of historical persons for future generations to learn from as if they were in the same room. Outside of the library, a patron using AR technology could look at the building and be presented with information on upcoming classes and new book releases. AR even has the opportunity to change how we read books—transforming both fiction and nonfiction texts into an interactive and more meaningful experience. AR can provide the reader with additional relevant digital content such as images, audio and video clips, or games throughout the text (without disturbing other patrons!).[35] The possibilities are limited only by the imagination.

One of the most intriguing aspects of AR in libraries is the potential for book displays and general presentation. Patrons will be able to perceive objects, information, details, and models based on local surroundings. For example, they could look at a shelf of books and see reviews, synopses, author biographies, and more, without typing a word. As staff at the New Mexico State University ask, "How would you like to stand at the end of a stack of books, hold up your phone, and look through an app to tell you where exactly the book is on the shelf?"[36] In this world, book displays might rapidly evolve and become augmented beacons of knowledge.

Today, headsets are the optimal medium for experiencing AR, but this may transition to digitally augmented contact lenses a user could wear, making digital content available without bulk. In this way, AR content could be delivered seamlessly and could truly appear to exist in the real world. This could unveil possibilities we cannot yet perceive.

In the very distant future, AR may even get to the point where it is indistinguishable from real life. The next logical step after AR contact lenses would be to bypass the human eye entirely and stream content directly to the brain.

Although this sounds like science fiction, Tesla CEO Elon Musk is already investing in a company that aims to link the human brain with a computer.[37] No one knows exactly where the technology is headed, but the prospects are certainly thought-provoking.

In this chapter, we have focused on many of the positive benefits that AR technology can bring to libraries and beyond. However, it is important to keep in mind that any new technological implementation carries a level of risk, and libraries should properly prepare to protect themselves. This means having a way to prevent theft of equipment, defense against legal issues from users who may experience trauma, suitable time limits, proper staff training, and more. Although the technology itself is usually user-friendly, it is not always easy to incorporate into a library's services.

AR is a groundbreaking technology, and it is likely to shape the future world we live in. While the technology is still young at this point, it is likely to prosper in our lifetimes. There is an opportunity for libraries to jump on board early and help steer this innovative technology so that it serves the public interest. We are at the forefront of an awe-inspiring future, and it is exciting to witness this young technology evolve right before our eyes. Hopefully, libraries will embrace this knowledge and include AR in some way, shape, or form as part of their public services for all.

NOTES

1. *Merriam-Webster Dictionary*, "Augmented Reality," https://www.merriam-webster.com/dictionary/augmented%20reality.
2. Jason Hall, "How Augmented Reality Is Changing the World of Consumer Marketing," 2017, https://www.forbes.com/sites/forbesagency council/2017/11/08/how-augmented-reality-is-changing-the-world-of-consumer-marketing/#31e4506d54cf.
3. Om Malik, "Pokémon Go Will Make You Crave Augmented Reality," 2016, https://www.newyorker.com/tech/elements/pokemon-go-will-make-you-crave-augmented-reality.
4. Siimon Reynolds, "Why Google Glass Failed: A Marketing Lesson," 2015, https://www.forbes.com/sites/siimonreynolds/2015/02/05/why-google-glass-failed/#395baf2e51b5.
5. Linda Lohr, "The Stereoscope: 3D for the 19th Century," 2015, libweb.lib.buffalo.edu/hslblog/history/?p=1512; Augment, "Infographic: The History of Augmented Reality," 2016, www.augment.com/blog/infographic-lengthy-history-augmented-reality/.
6. Dennis Williams II, "Did Sports Really Pave the Way for Augmented Reality?" 2016, https://www.huffingtonpost.com/entry/did-sports-really-pave-the-way-for-augmented-reality_us_57b4889be4b03dd53808f61d.
7. Joss Fong, "The NFL's Virtual First-Down Line, Explained," 2017, https://www.vox.com/2016/2/6/10919538/nfl-yellow-line.

8. Chris Isidore, "Fans' Bottom-Line Loss," 2001, money.cnn.com/2001/10/16/companies/column_sportsbiz/.

9. Cheryl V. Jackson, "How Libraries Are Using Technology to 'Stay up to Speed' with Patrons," 2015, www.chicagotribune.com/bluesky/originals/chi-american-library-association-meeting-bsi-20150205-story.html.

10. Elizabeth Zak, "Do You Believe in Magic? Exploring the Conceptualization of Augmented Reality and Its Implications for the User in the Field of Library and Information Science," *Information Technology and Libraries*, 2014, https://ejournals.bc.edu/ojs/index.php/ital/article/view/5638.

11. Daniel L. Ireton, Joelle Pitts, and Benjamin Ward, "Library Discovery through Augmented Reality: A Game Plan for Academics," Technology Collection, 2014, ijt.cgpublisher.com/product/pub.42/prod.965.

12. Zak, "Do You Believe in Magic?" 2014, https://ejournals.bc.edu/ojs/index.php/ital/article/view/5638.

13. Diana Hellyar, "Guest Post: Diana Hellyar on Library Use of New Visualization Technologies," 2016, informatics.mit.edu/blog/guest-post-diana-hellyar-library-use-new-visualization-technologies.

14. Hellyar, "Guest Post: Diana Hellyar on Library Use," 2016, informatics.mit.edu/blog/guest-post-diana-hellyar-library-use-new-visualization-technologies.

15. Heidi Brett, "Augmented Reality Is a Reality," 2017, https://attheu.utah.edu/facultystaff/augmented-reality-is-a-reality/.

16. NCSU Libraries, "Virtual Reality & Augmented Reality," https://www.lib.ncsu.edu/do/virtual-reality.

17. Michael Schaub, "'Pokémon Go' Sends Swarms of Players to Bookstores and Libraries. But Will They Remember the Books?" 2016, www.latimes.com/books/la-et-jc-pokemon-go-books-20160713-snap-htmlstory.html.

18. Adario Strange, "Oculus Installing Free VR Systems in Nearly 100 California Libraries," Mashable, 2017, mashable.com/2017/06/07/oculus-rift-library-project/.

19. White Plains Public Library, 2018, https://whiteplainslibrary.org.

20. Sandra Harrison, *White Plains, New York: A City of Contrasts* (Lulu, 2014).

21. White Plains Public Library, "Our Mission," 2018, https://whiteplainslibrary.org/policies/mission/.

22. Rob LeFebvre, "Microsoft's Next-Gen HoloLens Reportedly Won't Arrive until 2019," 2017, https://www.engadget.com/2017/02/20/next-gen-hololens-2019/.

23. Amber Wang, "Quiver Is the 3D Augmented Reality Coloring App for Adults," 2017, https://www.gearbrain.com/quiver-3d-coloring-app-review-2514323764.html.

24. Joseph Volpe, "Microsoft's HoloLens Is Now Ready for Developers," 2016, https://www.engadget.com/2016/02/29/microsoft-hololens-developer-preorders/.

25. Blake Morgan, "Augmented Reality and the Fourth Transformation," 2017, https://www.forbes.com/sites/blakemorgan/2017/11/30/augmented-reality -and-the-4th-transformation/#7cbece8d4bb3.
26. Robert Ferris, "Alibaba-Backed Augmented Reality Start-Up Makes Driving Look like a Video Game," 2017, https://www.cnbc.com/2017/11/28/wayray -uses-augmented-reality-to-turn-driving-into-a-video-game.html.
27. Association for Psychological Science, "Augmented-Reality Technology Could Help Treat 'Lazy Eye,'" Science Daily, 2017, https://www.sciencedaily.com/ releases/2017/12/171205115939.htm.
28. Brian Boyles, "Virtual Reality and Augmented Reality in Education," 2017, https://www.usma.edu/cfe/Literature/Boyles_17.pdf.
29. Jeremy Riel, "Augmented Reality in the Classroom," 2016, education.uic.edu/ academics-admissions/student-life/augmented-reality-classroom.
30. Joshua Bolkan, "Virtual and Augmented Reality to Nearly Double Each Year through 2021," 2017, https://thejournal.com/articles/2017/12/04/virtual -and-augmented-reality-to-nearly-double-each-year-through-2021.aspx.
31. Jonathan Vanian, "Amazon Takes a Trip in Virtual and Augmented Reality," 2017, fortune.com/2017/11/27/amazon-virtual-reality-augmented -sumerian/.
32. Lucas Matney, "Apple Acquired Augmented Reality Headset Startup Vrvana for $30M," 2017, https://techcrunch.com/2017/11/21/apple-acquires-mixed -reality-headset-startup-vrvana-for-30m/.
33. Seth Fiegerman, "Google Glass Is Back, with a New Vision," 2017, money.cnn .com/2017/07/18/technology/gadgets/google-glass-returns/index.html.
34. Forbes Agency Council, "13 Ways Augmented Reality Technology Can Work to Your Advantage," 2017, https://www.forbes.com/sites/forbesagencycoun cil/2017/11/16/13-ways-augmented-reality-technology-can-work-to-your -advantage/#29e7e0cc257a.
35. Yariv Levski, "10 Augmented Reality Books That Will Blow Your Kid's Mind," https://appreal-vr.com/blog/10-best-augmented-reality-books/.
36. Aggie Librarians NMSU, "Augmented Reality," 2014, lib.nmsu.edu/liblog/ augmented-reality/.
37. Alex Heath, "Elon Musk Has Raised $27 Million to Link Human Brains with Computers," 2017, www.businessinsider.com/elon-musk-neuralink-raises -27-million-2017–8.

BIBLIOGRAPHY

Aggie Librarians NMSU. "Augmented Reality." Last modified February 25, 2014. lib.nmsu.edu/liblog/augmented-reality/.

Association for Psychological Science. "Augmented-Reality Technology Could Help Treat 'Lazy Eye.'" Science Daily. 2017. https://www.sciencedaily.com/releases/ 2017/12/171205115939.htm.

Augment. "Infographic: The History of Augmented Reality." Last modified May 12, 2016. www.augment.com/blog/infographic-lengthy-history-augmented -reality/.

Bolkan, Joshua. "Virtual and Augmented Reality to Nearly Double Each Year through 2021." Last modified December 4, 2017. https://thejournal.com/ articles/2017/12/04/virtual-and-augmented-reality-to-nearly-double-each -year-through-2021.aspx.

Boyles, Brian. "Virtual Reality and Augmented Reality in Education." 2017. https:// www.usma.edu/cfe/Literature/Boyles_17.pdf.

Brett, Heidi. "Augmented Reality Is a Reality." Last modified March 20, 2017. https:// attheu.utah.edu/facultystaff/augmented-reality-is-a-reality/.

Ferris, Robert. "Alibaba-Backed Augmented Reality Start-Up Makes Driving Look like a Video Game." Last modified November 28, 2017. https://www.cnbc.com/ 2017/11/28/wayray-uses-augmented-reality-to-turn-driving-into-a-video-game .html.

Fiegerman, Seth. "Google Glass Is Back, with a New Vision." Last modified July 18, 2017. money.cnn.com/2017/07/18/technology/gadgets/google-glass-returns/ index.html.

Fong, Joss. "The NFL's Virtual First-Down Line, Explained." Last modified January 23, 2017. https://www.vox.com/2016/2/6/10919538/nfl-yellow-line.

Forbes Agency Council. "13 Ways Augmented Reality Technology Can Work to Your Advantage." Last modified November 11, 2017. https://www.forbes.com/sites/ forbesagencycouncil/2017/11/16/13-ways-augmented-reality-technology-can -work-to-your-advantage/#29e7e0cc257a.

Hall. Jason. "How Augmented Reality Is Changing the World of Consumer Marketing." Last modified November 8, 2017. https://www.forbes.com/sites/ forbesagencycouncil/2017/11/08/how-augmented-reality-is-changing-the -world-of-consumer-marketing/#31e4506d54cf.

Harrison, Sandra. *White Plains, New York: A City of Contrasts*. Lulu, 2014.

Heath, Alex. "Elon Musk Has Raised $27 Million to Link Human Brains with Computers." Last modified August 25, 2017. www.businessinsider.com/elon -musk-neuralink-raises-27-million-2017–8.

Hellyar, Diana. "Guest Post: Diana Hellyar on Library Use of New Visualization Technologies." Last modified April 26, 2016. informatics.mit.edu/blog/guest -post-diana-hellyar-library-use-new-visualization-technologies.

HTC Vive. "Vive." https://www.vive.com/us/.

Ireton, Daniel L., Joelle Pitts, and Benjamin Ward. "Library Discovery through Augmented Reality: A Game Plan for Academics." Technology Collection. 2014. ijt.cgpublisher.com/product/pub.42/prod.965.

Isidore, Chris. "Fans' Bottom-Line Loss." Last modified October 16, 2001. money.cnn .com/2001/10/16/companies/column_sportsbiz/.

Jackson, Cheryl V. "How Libraries Are Using Technology to 'Stay Up to Speed' with Patrons." Last modified February 6, 2015. www.chicagotribune.com/bluesky/originals/chi-american-library-association-meeting-bsi-20150205-story.html.

LeFebvre, Rob. "Microsoft's Next-Gen HoloLens Reportedly Won't Arrive until 2019." Last modified February 20, 2017. https://www.engadget.com/2017/02/20/next-gen-hololens-2019/.

Levski, Yariv. "10 Augmented Reality Books That Will Blow Your Kid's Mind." https://appreal-vr.com/blog/10-best-augmented-reality-books/.

Lohr, Linda. "The Stereoscope: 3D for the 19th Century." libweb.lib.buffalo.edu/hslblog/history/?p=1512.

Malik, Om. "Pokémon Go Will Make You Crave Augmented Reality." Last modified July 12, 2016. https://www.newyorker.com/tech/elements/pokemon-go-will-make-you-crave-augmented-reality.

Matney, Lucas. "Apple Acquired Augmented Reality Headset Startup Vrvana for $30M." Last modified November 12, 2017. https://techcrunch.com/2017/11/21/apple-acquires-mixed-reality-headset-startup-vrvana-for-30m/.

Merriam-Webster Dictionary. "Augmented Reality." https://www.merriam-webster.com/dictionary/augmented%20reality.

Morgan, Blake. "Augmented Reality and the Fourth Transformation." Last modified November 30, 2017. https://www.forbes.com/sites/blakemorgan/2017/11/30/augmented-reality-and-the-4th-transformation/#7cbece8d4bb3.

NCSU Libraries. "Virtual Reality & Augmented Reality." https://www.lib.ncsu.edu/do/virtual-reality.

Oculus Rift. "Oculus." https://www.oculus.com/rift/.

Reynolds, Siimon. "Why Google Glass Failed: A Marketing Lesson." Last modified February 5, 2015. https://www.forbes.com/sites/siimonreynolds/2015/02/05/why-google-glass-failed/#395baf2e51b5.

Riel, Jeremy. "Augmented Reality in the Classroom." Last modified March 7, 2016. education.uic.edu/academics-admissions/student-life/augmented-reality-classroom.

Schaub, Michael. "'Pokémon Go' Sends Swarms of Players to Bookstores and Libraries. But Will They Remember the Books?" Last modified July 13, 2016. www.latimes.com/books/la-et-jc-pokemon-go-books-20160713-snap-htmlstory.html.

Strange, Adario. "Oculus Installing Free VR Systems in Nearly 100 California Libraries." Mashable. Last modified June 7, 2017. mashable.com/2017/06/07/oculus-rift-library-project/.

Vanian, Jonathan. "Amazon Takes a Trip in Virtual and Augmented Reality." Last modified November 27, 2017. fortune.com/2017/11/27/amazon-virtual-reality-augmented-sumerian/.

Volpe, Joseph. "Microsoft's HoloLens Is Now Ready for Developers." Last modified February 29, 2016. https://www.engadget.com/2016/02/29/microsoft-hololens -developer-preorders/.

Wang, Amber. "Quiver Is the 3D Augmented Reality Coloring App for Adults." Last modified December 4, 2017. https://www.gearbrain.com/quiver-3d-coloring -app-review-2514323764.html.

White Plains Public Library. "Our Mission." https://whiteplainslibrary.org/policies/ mission/.

Williams II, Dennis. "Did Sports Really Pave the Way for Augmented Reality?" Last modified August 17, 2016. https://www.huffingtonpost.com/entry/did-sports -really-pave-the-way-for-augmented-reality_us_57b4889be4b03dd53808f61d.

Zak, Elizabeth. "Do You Believe in Magic? Exploring the Conceptualization of Augmented Reality and Its Implications for the User in the Field of Library and Information Science." *Information Technology and Libraries*, 2014. https:// ejournals.bc.edu/ojs/index.php/ital/article/view/5638.

CHAD M. CLARK

2

Extended Reality in Informal Learning Environments

THE IDEA OF BEING ABLE TO INHABIT A VIRTUAL WORLD AND INTER-act with objects has been around for decades.[1] Within the purview of pedagogy, it has long been thought that virtual reality (VR), once raised from its developmental phase to greater accessibility, could afford opportunities to experience environments which, for reasons of time, distance, scale, and safety, would not otherwise be available to many people.[2] Recent breakthroughs in immersive technologies, as well as an increase in semi-affordable devices on the market, have helped expand VR's applications to research beyond the military and scientific visualization realm into more multidisciplinary areas, such as education, art, and psychology.[3] In many ways, libraries are at an intersection of these disciplines. In this chapter, I will discuss what my library has done to serve as a neutral area and informal learning environment for people to come together and learn how the new immersive technology may fit into their fields of interest.

EMPOWERING ACROSS CONTEXTS

I am a new media librarian at the Highland Park Public Library (HPPL) in Highland Park, Illinois, located ten miles north of Chicago. Our library serves a population of approximately 30,000 people of every age, income level, ethnicity, and physical ability, and provides a full range of information resources needed to live, learn, work, and govern. As the center of expertise regarding information technology, HPPL leads in exploring and enabling new technologies to empower our community. At HPPL, as well as in this chapter, we refer to anyone who attends the library's learning workshops or utilizes its resources as a "student."

HPPL first became interested in virtual reality in March 2015. That year I had the opportunity to attend the South by South West Interactive Festival in Austin, Texas, as a representative of the library. There I attended a workshop led by Brian Chirls, a creative technologist based in New York and an expert in immersive design. The workshop revolved around a web tool that Chirls had recently developed in response to his own observations that, while it is possible to *experience* VR content at an entry level on a relatively low budget, the pathways to *creating* VR content are filled with obstacles.[4]

Chirls reasoned that (1) even with inexpensive VR viewers such as Google Cardboard, designers still need expensive software and hardware for VR content creation; (2) most people lack the educational resources or experience to program three-dimensional environments and manage the intricacies of head-tracking and VR display technology; and (3) a form of distribution is needed for VR content creation; that is, a web hosting or content delivery network service from which to deliver the media and program files. If the VR field were to be broadened into a truly diverse and innovative range of material, Chirls emphasized, it needed to make creation as accessible as consumption.

At the workshop, Chirls then introduced his project titled the WebVR Starter Kit, a tool he created demonstrating that VR content could, in fact, be made with limited resources and technical skills. As a technology-focused librarian serving lifelong learners in a public library, I became interested in the potential of this tool and the possibility of bringing VR to our community in a meaningful way.

After several weeks of researching the landscape of consumer VR products, my team and I made the decision to acquire and integrate several platforms that together we believed would provide a wide range of opportunities to engage, consume, and create data in three-dimensional environments. An important factor for us was having the ability to offer VR access to people with a diverse range of technical skill sets. The platforms we selected were HoloLens (Microsoft); a collection of open-source WebVR developer tools that include the WebVR Starter Kit (Chirls) and A-Frame (Mozilla); and Google Cardboard (Google). All of these platforms reside under the umbrella of reality technologies, but it is worth outlining their fundamental similarities and differences in order to better understand how and why they can be integrated into informal learning environments.

COMBINED ENVIRONMENTS

The recent growth of new devices and content is at least partially responsible for the fact that the terminology surrounding VR technologies has become, to some extent, unclear.[5] From a consumer's perspective, the labels applied to VR technologies may appear in some instances to be synonymous, while others are very different. Augmented reality (AR), virtual reality (VR), and mixed reality (MR) all seek to change the way we perceive and interact with our physical, real-world reality, but what is it that sets them apart from each other?

The extent to which reality is replaced by virtual elements is a useful benchmark in distinguishing VR, AR, and MR from each other. *Virtual reality* is a completely artificial environment that is created with software and is presented to the user in such a way that the user suspends belief and accepts it as a real environment.[6] *Augmented reality* is an overlay of content on the real world, but that content is not anchored to or part of it.[7] Real-world content and AR-generated content are not able to respond to each other. In a *mixed reality* experience, physical and digital objects coexist and interact in real time.[8] Mixed reality is an overlay of content on the real world, and that content is anchored to or part of it. Real-world content and MR-generated content can respond to each other. Contrary to a VR experience where the user is immersed in a completely different world, MR experiences invite digital content into the user's real-world surroundings, allowing interaction between the two in real time. These interactions mimic natural behavior, such as objects getting bigger as you get closer and perspectives changing as the user moves around an object.

In 1994, Paul Milgram and Fumio Kishino devised a spectrum they called Extended Reality (XR) to explain the relationship of AR and VR. On one end is physical reality, and on the other is a fully visualized digital world (see figure 2.1).[9] XR essentially includes all the environments created for human and machine interactions that combine the real and virtual worlds. *XR* is a far-reaching, inclusive, and flexible term. The "X" in XR represents a variable

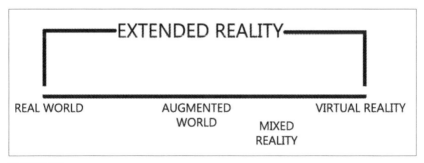

FIGURE 2.1

Extended reality

that is not fully known or specified, intentionally suggesting an open ecosystem that stakeholders hope will expand. Many industries (news media, health care, motion pictures, retail, and marketing) are beginning to embrace the term *XR* based on projections that immersive technologies will continue to mature, and expectations that moving from VR to AR or MR will one day be a single seamless experience.[10]

CASE PLATFORMS

The following platforms were implemented at my library so that we could provide VR access to people with a diverse range of technical skill sets in an informal learning environment. Brief definitions of each platform are provided to delineate the differences in interaction models and capabilities between them. *Specifications* describe the physical properties of each platform, or as is the case with WebVR Kit, the foundational API that provides code to build VR solutions for the Web. *Control* describes the aspects of each platform that enable movement through virtual environment.

HoloLens

Specifications: Microsoft's HoloLens is a self-contained, head-mount display (HMD) holographic computer that enables users to engage with digital content and interact with holograms in the world around them.[11] It is equipped with see-through holographic high-definition lenses that use an advanced optical projection system to generate multidimensional full-color images. HoloLens operates by mapping the user's physical environment and creating a 3D plot of his or her surroundings. The process of mapping real-world surfaces into the virtual world is known as spatial mapping.[12] HoloLens uses spatial mapping to determine exactly where and how to place digital content into that space—realistically—while allowing users to interact with it using gestures.[13]

Control: Physical gestures allow users to take action while wearing the HoloLens. HoloLens recognizes three core gestures that they call Air Tap, Gaze, and Bloom. Air Tap is a tapping gesture with the hand held upright, like a mouse click or select. This is used in most HoloLens experiences for the equivalent of a "click" on a UI element after targeting it with Gaze. Gaze is a gesture that involves head movement and is used to move the cursor to highlight holographic objects for selection. When a holographic object is ready to select, it will be highlighted. Bloom is the "home" gesture and is reserved for that alone. It is a special system action that is used to go back to the Start Menu. Bloom is performed by holding out a hand with the palm up and fingertips held together and then opening the hand. Holographic objects can also be selected by speaking the voice command "Select."

Google Cardboard

Specifications: Google Cardboard is a VR platform that was developed by Google for use with a head mount for a smartphone. The parts that make up a Cardboard viewer are a piece of cardboard cut into a precise shape, 45-mm focal-length lenses, magnets or capacitive tape, a hook and loop fastener (such as Velcro), a rubber band, and an optional near field communication (NFC) tag.[14] The platform is intended as a low-cost system to encourage interest and development in VR applications.

Control: Google Cardboard works by placing a smartphone at the optimal distance away from the lenses. Then, by using compatible apps, the lenses create a 3D effect when held up to your eyes. Users can even move their head around, and the images will respond as if they are in the same place as what is displayed on the screen. Official Google Cardboards (do-it-yourself versions are also available) come with an NFC chip that will automatically launch the official Cardboard app when users place their phones into the headset. On the side of the viewer is a button that is in fact a magnet. When pressed, it acts as if the user has physically pressed the screen on the smartphone. This is Google's way of leveraging the phone's magnetometer, which is usually reserved for compass functions.

WebVR Kit

Specifications: WebVR is an open specification that makes it possible to experience VR in your browser. The WebVR Starter Kit serves as a rapid VR prototyping for creative authors without advanced technical skills. It consists of a single JavaScript file that, when included in a web page, bootstraps an empty virtual reality scene. WebVR Starter Kit includes an API[15] that wraps three.js[16] in simplified commands for creating and manipulating simple 3D objects in an empty scene displayed on a web page. The API is targeted toward the level of coding skill taught on a site like Codeacademy and was inspired by Vidcode, a project for teaching girls how to code with video and image processing. The resulting web page adapts to a range of devices, whether it runs on an iOS or Android phone with Cardboard, an Oculus Rift, or on a 2D monitor. It can be hosted for free on an HTML/JavaScript sandbox site like JS Bin.[17]

Control: The API covers the basics of building a scene, as well as the means to make it dynamic and interactive. Users can create and manipulate "primitive" shapes (box, sphere, torus, cylinder, etc.). They can apply textures (metal, stone, grass, etc.) to these shapes, or custom textures via an image file. With a smartphone, users can create backgrounds based on the 360-degree spherical photos.[18] Users can also import media (2D images, audio) and trigger events such as media playback, object animation, or phone vibration.

HOLOLENS AND COLLABORATIVE VISUALIZATION SPACE

HoloLens developers are already beginning to introduce potentially new approaches to data visualization.[19] Data visualization is a very broad discipline that encompasses several different fields; for instance, information visualization aims to find new paradigms to efficiently display huge amounts of data (e.g., the network traffic over the Internet), whereas scientific visualization aims to present users with phenomena that are very hard (or impossible) to perceive (e.g., the airflow around a plane wing).[20] The intrinsic nature of XR technologies provides collaborative visualization with a worthwhile tool to display virtual objects within a physical space; moreover, Microsoft is spending considerable research and resources to bring the emerging applications for visualization to the HoloLens.

HoloAnatomy

HoloAnatomy is a HoloLens app that enables viewers to examine the organs of a body at their own pace and from any perspective. The HoloLens projects holographic objects into the user's field of view, mixing virtual with physical and essentially enhancing our understanding of the human body. At the Highland Park Public Library, we partner with an outside organization that presents nutrition programs at the library. At the end of each program, we give attendees an opportunity to explore whole biological systems via the HoloLens. We have also embedded HoloAnatomy in our stacks by displaying signage near our medical texts that encourages students to access the HoloLens and experience the HoloAnatomy app.

Minecraft

During our Minecraft workshops, we use the HoloLens to introduce collaborative visualization to a younger generation. Minecraft, which is a popular virtual environment, requires an adequate amount of spatial thinking to successfully navigate. Spatial thinking is thinking that finds meaning in the shape, size, orientation, location, and direction or trajectory of objects, or the relative positions in space of multiple objects.[21] Using a program called Mineways[22] in combination with the HoloLens, we devised a way for gamers to visualize their Minecraft creations as holograms (see figure 2.2). Our librarians teach gamers how to select a volume in their Minecraft world, export it to an OBJ file,[23] and then upload the OBJ to a HoloLens app called HoloStudio.[24] Through this process, we have observed gamers viewing, discussing, and critiquing their work in ways they never could before. Gamers have expressed to librarians how they have gained fresh insight and been able to fix problems more effectively. They have also expressed satisfaction with being able to bring

FIGURE 2.2
Minecraft model rendered in HoloLens

their designs out of screen space and into real space, where they could interact with their models and evaluate their creation in another context.

imrsv.data

imrsv.data is a HoloLens app that can be used to visualize any JSON/CSV file (given that it conforms to a certain format) as a three-dimensional bar graph. For several years our library has partnered with a network of volunteer, expert business mentors who meet with students on a regular basis at the library. Recently, library staff have begun attending these meetings and allowing interested students to view Excel spreadsheets through the HoloLens. The purpose is to have group members examine the way that they use and see data, and promote discussion about this. Students have responded that in some cases, the additional dimension allowed for differences in size to be perceived more clearly. Students also noted how more data could be displayed at the same time because data points can be placed among three dimensions. More data simultaneously visualized in a comprehensible form could facilitate data analysis and pattern recognition.[25]

VR CONTENT CREATION IN THE OPEN WEB

VR content creation in the open web is in the experimental phase, and fittingly for informal learning environments, there is room to play. Most conversations about VR surround specific headsets, like HoloLens, Oculus Rift, or Google Daydream. But technologies are also emerging that can bring immersive experiences to any device with a modern web browser. Open standards for VR and web compatibility are being created that allow students to build a seemingly endless variety of VR experiences with surprisingly limited skill sets and resources.[26]

WebVR Starter Kit

WebVR Starter Kit is a VR content creation tool consisting of a single JavaScript file that bootstraps an empty virtual reality scene. It includes an API that wraps three.js in simplified commands for creating and manipulating simple 3D objects in that empty scene. At HPPL, WebVR Starter Kit has proven to be a useful tool for introducing students with various skill set levels to the basic framework of creating VR content. Equally important, we feel, the kit demonstrates to students a story-telling power they may not have been aware of previously that can be used to engage people with their ideas.

Staff members facilitate two-hour workshops for groups of 5–10 students using WebVR Starter Kit to demonstrate the VR environment in a hands-on setting. Each participant is equipped with a laptop (their own or one of ours) that is connected to the Internet. To provide a web page that each participant can edit right in the browser, we guide them to jsbin.com and have them set up an account. It is not necessary to make an account to use JS Bin, but we encourage it because students' work will eventually expire without one. Once on jsbin.com, students are then shown how to paste the WebVR Starter Kit script in the HTML panel and how to begin coding by referring to a list of commands.

Students are then given a list of WebVR Starter Kit commands and led through a series of exercises that show them what they can do in just a few lines of code. These exercises include the following ones: Panorama (creating a spherical panoramic photo); Sound (creating audio sources in 3D space); Animation (creating a simple animation, moving and rotating objects); Sky

```
VR.floor().setMaterial('grass')
VR.sky()
VR.video(['https://povdocs
  .github.io/webvr-starter-kit/
  examples/assets/bigbuckbur
```

FIGURE 2.3
WebVR Starter Kit

```
VR.floor().setMaterial('wood');

VR.sky();
```

FIGURE 2.4

Indicating a wooden floor and a sky with two lines of code

```
VR.box({color:'green'}).moveTo(0,2,0)

VR.text('This is my cylinder').moveTo(0,1,0)
```

FIGURE 2.5

Indicating color and position

(creating a realistic daytime sky with movable sun and lighting); and Near and Far (creating actions triggered when an object moves closer to or farther away from the viewer). WebVR Starter Kit offers a library of predefined materials for texture maps, like grass, stone, metal, and wood. The simplicity of the WebVR Starter Kit is highlighted in figure 2.3, which was created with only three lines of code.

After students are taught how to add objects in a VR environment, they are shown how to add attributes to them like position, color, material, and simple animation. For example, students can indicate that they want a wooden floor and a sky with two lines of code (see figure 2.4), or they can add a green cylinder, position it, and indicate that it is theirs (see figure 2.5).

At the halfway point of the workshop, after students have become familiar with the VR environment, instructors distribute Google Cardboards. Each student's JS Bin URL automatically adapts to a range of devices, whether it runs on an iOS or Android phone, with cardboard. We encourage students to share their JS Bin URL with others and go back to it later to continue editing, or to "fork" the code to a new URL. Finally, we recommend to any students who are interested in continuing to explore VR content creation to attend our next-level workshop, which is titled A-Frame with HTML.

A-Frame with HTML

A-Frame, like WebVR Starter Kit, is a way to develop VR content in the open web. Mozilla built A-Frame as an easier way to create content on top of their pioneering WebVR platform.[27] Now, as an independent open-source project, A-Frame has grown to be one of the largest VR communities.

A-Frame can be developed from a plain HTML file without having to install anything, and it can be used to create VR experiences that run on any WebGL-enabled[28] browser or VR headset. The idea behind A-Frame is to make it possible to create VR scenes using HTML tags and properties, essentially making the VR development process like building a website. A good example of a VR experience made using A-Frame is the *Washington Post*'s article "Mars:

An Interactive Journey" (www.washingtonpost.com/graphics/business/mars -journey/).

During our A-Frame with HTML workshops, instructors teach students how to modify objects through HTML attributes. In HTML, an attribute is a characteristic of a page element, such as font size or color. As a jumping-off point, students are shown how to begin experimenting immediately with A-Frame by remixing A-Frame projects on Glitch.com. Glitch.com is an online code editor that hosts and deploys web projects for free. Workshop instructors lead students through remix lessons that are built into Glitch.com. These lessons demonstrate how to locate and change the position of objects in 3D space (X, Y, Z), change colors, apply rotations, and alter scale. After the Glitch.com lessons have been completed, students are shown how to create more complex 3D elements in MagicaVoxel[29] and then how to import them into A-Frame.

Storytelling with Guri

Guri, developed by Dan Zajdband, is a set of tools focused on the creation of VR experiences based on intuitive descriptions. Unlike our WebVR Starter Kit and A-Frame for HTML workshops, our Storytelling with Guri workshops do not involve any coding. The primary tool is the editor, which allows users to express in plain English what they want to experience. All projects made in Guri generate an embeddable link for sharing the student's VR scene. The output is an HTML file using auto-generated A-Frame markup.

During our Guri workshops students are shown how to navigate the editor, which can be found at GuriVR.com. The workshop begins by covering the basics of 360-degree photos and 3D modeling and then progresses into mixing these assets with audio to create immersive stories. By the end of the workshop, students leave with a finished VR experience that they can use and share directly from the Web with any device.

IMPLICATIONS FOR THE FUTURE DIRECTION OF XR TECHNOLOGIES IN LIBRARIES

Historically, libraries have included in their functions the creation, as well as the preservation and dissemination, of content in many different formats.[30] As librarians, we are just beginning to look at how VR technology will impact the way our visitors think and process information—and how we can integrate the technology into the instructional and learning process.

Libraries and shared academic spaces may someday provide physical grids or open sound stages designed for virtual interaction, where groups of students may take guided field trips to remote sites, interface with other cultures, or travel in time.[31] And the instructor may be there as well, guiding the conversation, pointing out important concepts and features, and posing questions.

Students with physical disabilities or financial disadvantages may have access to places and experiences they never had before. The ability to experience things that could only be theorized about before, such as journeying into a black hole or flying through a strand of DNA, is already becoming possible for students.[32]

VARlibraries[33] began installing VR systems in public libraries in California in 2016. VARlibraries reports that they are working with the California state librarian and CALIFA to make immersive learning available and accessible to people through libraries, in an equitable distribution of what Mark Zuckerberg says is "the next computing platform" of the twenty-first century.[34]

Since the ubiquity of smartphones is now making it possible for libraries and other cultural institutions to provide XR applications that allow people to explore collections in new and exciting ways,[35] introducing XR does not require having a lot of infrastructure in place. It is more about building partnerships, making these consumer technologies accessible to library visitors, and providing resources and time for staff to get up to speed. Training staff to navigate XR technologies continues the library's tradition of democratizing access to technology.

As society continues to experiment with new applications for XR, the possibility of censorship is a growing concern.[36] If the distribution of XR apps is dependent on proprietary sources, then a handful of companies can restrict content based upon their own preferences and sensibilities. This may mean that XR experiences that explore contentious topics would not be accessible. There are no such restrictions on the Web in the United States, at least as of 2018,[37] which is why libraries should be a proponent of WebVR.

NOTES

1. Steven LaValle, *Virtual Reality* (London: Cambridge University Press, 2017), 5.
2. John Cromby, Penny Standen, and David Brown, "Using Virtual Environments in Special Education," VR in the Schools, 1995, www.hitl .washington.edu/projects/knowledge_base/virtual-worlds/VR-in-Schools/.
3. Keith Curtin, "Mixed Reality Will Be Most Important Tech of 2017," The Next Web, https://thenextweb.com/insider/2017/01/07/mixed-reality-will -be-most-important-tech-of-2017/#.tnw_KbVD0Lvs.
4. Brian Chirls, "How Anyone Can Create a Virtual Reality Experience with One Line of Code," *Point of View's Documentary Blog,* www.pbs.org/pov/blog/ povdocs/2015/02/how-anyone-can-create-virtual-reality-experiences-with -one-line-of-code/#.VRvXVZPF91Q.
5. Paul Armstrong, "Just How Big Is the Virtual Reality Market and Where Is It Going Next?" *Forbes,* https://www.forbes.com/sites/paularmstrongtech/ 2017/04/06/just-how-big-is-the-virtual-reality-market-and-where-is-it -going-next/#2abb2b304834.
6. John Pullen, "Everything to Know about Virtual Reality," *Time,* http://time .com/4122253/virtual-reality/.

7. Dieter Schmalstieg and Tobias Höllerer, *Augmented Reality: Principles and Practice* (Boston: Addison-Wesley, 2016), 64.

8. Brian Shuster, "Virtual Reality and Learning: The Newest Landscape for Higher Education," *Wired,* August 6, 2015, https://www.wired.com/insights/ 2013/12virtual-reality-and-learning-the-newest-landscape-for -higher-education/.

9. Paul Milgram, "Augmented Reality: A Class of Displays on the Reality-Virtuality Continuum," Telemanipulator and Telepresence Technologies, http://etclab.mie.utoronto.ca/publication/1994/Milgram_Takemura _SPIE1994.pdf.

10. Linda Lian, "XR Is a New Way to Consider the Reality Continuum," TechCrunch, https://techcrunch.com/2017/05/02/xr-a-new-way-to-consider -the-reality-continuum/.

11. Matt Zeller, "Windows Dev Center," https://docs.microsoft.com/en-us/ windows/mixed-reality/hololens-hardware-details.

12. Woodrow Barfield and Claudia Hendrix, "The Effect of Update Rate on the Sense of Presence within Virtual Environments," *Virtual Reality: The Journal of the Virtual Reality Society* 1, no. 1 (1995): 3–16, https://doi.org/10.1007/ BF02009709.

13. Zeller, "Windows Dev Center," https://docs.microsoft.com/en-us/windows/ mixed-reality/hololens-hardware-details.

14. Near-field communication (NFC) is a set of communication protocols that enable two electronic devices, one of which is usually a portable device such as a smartphone, to establish communication by bringing them within 4 cm (1.6 inches) of each other.

15. API is the acronym for application programming interface, which is a software intermediary that allows two applications to talk to each other.

16. Three.js is a cross-browser JavaScript library and application programming interface that is used to create and display animated 3D computer graphics in a web browser.

17. JS Bin (jsbin.com) is an HTML/JavaScript sandbox that enables users to learn, experiment, and teach using web technologies.

18. A 360-degree photo is a controllable panoramic image that surrounds the original point from which the shot was taken.

19. Michael Peters, "Videos and Discussion on Design and Development with the HoloLens," In-vivible.com, www.in-vizible.com/videoblog.html.

20. Mi Jeong Kim, "Implementing an Augmented Reality-Enabled Wayfinding System through Studying User Experience and Requirements in Complex Environments," *Visualization in Engineering,* https://viejournal.springeropen .com/articles/10.1186/s40327–015–0026–2.

21. Paul Pickering, "Sensor Fusion: Making Sense of the Real World for IoT Applications," *Electronic Component News,* https://www.ecnmag.com/ article/2016/02/sensor-fusion-making-sense-real-world-iot-applications.

22. Mineways is an open-source file exporter for rendering, 3D printing, and schematic creation and viewing.

23. OBJ is an open geometry definition file format that has been adopted by many 3D graphics application vendors.

24. HoloStudio is a HoloLens app for creating, sharing, and 3D-printing your own holograms.

25. Christopher M. Bishop, *Pattern Recognition and Machine Learning* (New York: Springer. 2006), 164–71.

26. Stuart Dredge, "The Complete Guide to Virtual Reality—Everything You Need to Get Started," *The Guardian,* https://www.theguardian.com/technology/2016/nov/10/virtual-reality-guide-headsets-apps-games-vr.

27. WebVR is an open specification that makes it possible to experience VR in a web browser. Its purpose is to make it easier for everyone to access VR experiences, regardless of the device they own.

28. WebGL (Web Graphics Library) is a JavaScript API for rendering interactive 2D and 3D graphics within any compatible web browser without the use of plug-ins.

29. Magica Voxel is a free 8-bit voxel art editor and interactive path-tracing renderer.

30. American Library Association, https://www.ala.org.

31. Andrea Moneta, "How Virtual Reality Is Changing the Way We Experience Stage Shows," The Conversation, http://theconversation.com/how-virtual-reality-is-changing-the-way-we-experience-stage-shows-81542.

32. Graeme Lawrie, "How Our School Is Using Virtual Reality to Prepare Pupils for a Future Dominated by Technology," *The Telegraph,* https://www.telegraph.co.uk/education/2017/01/23/school-using-virtual-reality-prepare-pupils-future-dominated/.

33. VARlibraries is a national network of libraries that are implementing virtual and augmented reality technology in their communities.

34. Troy Lambert, "Virtual Reality in the Library: Creating a New Experience," Public Libraries Online, http://publiclibrariesonline.org/2016/02/virtual-reality-in-the-library-creating-a-new-experience/.

35. Ani Boyadjian, "Augmented Library," The Digital Shift, www.thedigitalshift.com/2014/09/mobile/augmented-library-technology/#.

36. Jack Smith, "Apple Censored an App about the Ferguson Shooting—Here's Why," Mic.com, https://mic.com/articles/125612/apple-censored-an-app-about-the-ferguson-shooting-ferguson-firsthand-heres-why#.xRc5GnFrv.

37. Jeff Sommer, "What Net Neutrality Rules Say," *New York Times,* https://www.nytimes.com/interactive/2015/03/12/technology/net-neutrality-rules-explained.html.

3

Virtual Reality for 3D Modeling

VIRTUAL REALITY HAS BEEN ATTRACTING MUCH ATTENTION OVER the last several years, but the release of the HTC Vive and the Oculus Rift, the two high-end VR systems, in 2016 finally brought the immersive 3D experience to the reach of the general public.[1] These VR systems with a 3D head-mounted display make it possible for people to experience and interact with the virtual digital world. The immersive VR environment can be a tremendous asset in multiple contexts such as learning, job training, product design, and prototyping. Once combined with conversational systems that provide an interface that uses voice as well as other modalities such as gesture, sight, and sound, VR is expected to become an even more powerful tool in the near future.[2]

Most people think that VR technology is for gaming and entertainment. But VR has the potential to impact many more areas and is quickly becoming a mainstream technology trend. Gartner, a research and consulting company, counted VR and augmented reality in its top ten strategic technology trends for 2018, maintaining that AR, VR, and mixed reality hold the potential to transform the current user experience into something invisible and immersive.[3] Another research and consulting firm, Deloitte, also believes that VR and AR technologies have reached a point where they can now go beyond the proof-of-concept stage and are ready to be applied to innovative use cases and prototypes for industrialization.[4]

VR, AR, and MR technologies are driving some exciting innovations in engineering, medicine, and education. For example, NASA's Jet Propulsion Laboratory developed a digital environment called ProtoSpace. This multicolored, computer-aided design (CAD) rendering mixed-reality program allows engineers to build an object that feels like a real object and to find flaws in the design before a physical part is built by combining virtual reality and augmented reality technologies.[5] Stryker, a medical and surgical equipment and technology company, has recently developed a mixed-reality interface for surgeons, called Scopis.[6] It uses Microsoft's HoloLens, a self-contained holographic computer and headset, and guides a surgeon through spinal and other complex surgeries with a medical image guidance system overlay in order to improve the accuracy and speed of the surgery.[7] In classrooms, teachers are introducing tools such as Google Expeditions and DiscoveryVR to bring the VR experience to students.[8]

Since 2011, when the Fayetteville Free Library in New York state created the first library makerspace in the United States, many libraries have set up makerspaces of their own to help library users to explore new technologies such as 3D printing. VR is a natural addition to a makerspace, which is closely associated with early exposure and equitable access to new technologies, hands-on activities, and experiential learning. In this chapter, I will discuss how VR can be incorporated into a library makerspace, particularly for the creation of 3D models, thereby empowering library patrons to become not only savvy consumers of 3D technology, but also active creators of 3D content.

WHY VIRTUAL REALITY FOR 3D MODELING?

One of the most commonly found items in a makerspace is a desktop 3D printer. People find it intriguing to watch a 3D printer build an object according to the design displayed on the computer. Once people see how the 3D printing process works, many of them also talk about what things they may want to design and 3D-print. For this reason, library programs about 3D printing are quite popular. Many who try 3D printing, however, soon realize that in order to take full advantage of the 3D printing technology, they need to become familiar not only with operating the 3D printer but also with 3D modeling. It is possible to use the 3D printing technology to simply 3D-print a model that has been downloaded online. But the real power of a 3D printer lies in its ability to take a custom-designed 3D model and turn it into a real object. Furthermore, even to simply 3D-print a preexisting 3D model, one needs to understand how 3D modeling works at a basic level. This is because not all 3D models have valid 3D geometry. For a 3D printer to successfully build a three-dimensional object, the model must be solid, meaning that all surfaces of the object are sealed and watertight.

3D model files, including those created with a 3D scanner, do not always accurately represent solid objects. In a computer, a 3D model is often represented by a mesh, which is a collection of vertices (points), edges (line segments connecting two vertices), and faces (a flat surface enclosed by edges).[9] This 3D mesh determines the surface shape of an object. It is entirely possible for a mesh to look like a three-dimensional object when displayed on the screen while it actually does not have the correct 3D geometry to be a solid object in the real world. This is the reason why a 3D model file that is sent to a 3D printer sometimes results in an error that prevents the 3D printer from creating the object. Such a 3D model is likely to contain a mesh error, such as open gaps (non-watertight surfaces), non-manifold edges (extra edges in a face), self-intersecting faces, and inverted triangles (surfaces facing the wrong direction), as illustrated in figure 3.1. A 3D model with any of these issues needs to be repaired using a 3D modeling software before it can be 3D-printed.[10]

In order to fix these errors, as well as to tweak an existing design or create a new model, a user needs to know how to use a 3D modeling application such as Blender, Google SketchUp, Rhino, SolidWorks, or Tinkercad.[11] Some of these applications are more basic than others. But none of them is easy for a novice to learn, and none of them are intuitive to use. Learning how to design

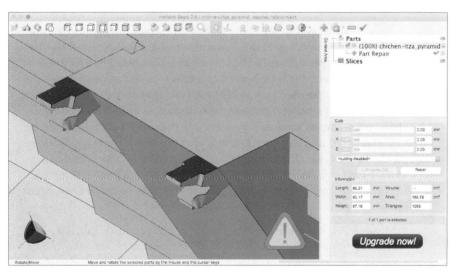

FIGURE 3.1

A 3D model with inverted triangles, which is a type of a mesh error, shown in NetFabb, a 3D modeling software. The inverted triangles are the two areas that appear dark.

a 3D model using these applications involves going through many tutorials, as well as using trial and error.

What a makerspace ultimately tries to achieve is growing more makers, and that includes educating people about not only how to operate a 3D printer, but also how to create 3D content.[12] When a 3D modeling application is hard to learn and difficult to use, this creates a barrier to growing more makers and helping them become familiar with 3D modeling. Designing or manipulating a three-dimensional object on a two-dimensional screen with a keyboard and a mouse is tricky. By contrast, in the VR environment, one is no longer restricted by two-dimensional interface and design tools. The VR environment makes handling and interacting with a 3D model a lot more intuitive and easier to learn. There are already a large number of 3D modeling and sculpting tools developed for the VR environment.[13] With these tools, libraries can show people how one can more easily and quickly create and modify a 3D model in the VR environment and eventually 3D-print it. The combination of a VR system, such as the HTC Vive or the Oculus Rift, a 3D printer, and related educational offerings can generate great synergy for a library makerspace.

VIRTUAL REALITY EQUIPMENT AND APPLICATIONS FOR 3D MODELING

Currently, the HTC Vive and the Oculus Rift are two popular high-end VR systems. Both of them consist of the headset, two controllers, and two sensors. The sensors and the headset are connected to the computer by cable, and the sensors track the position and the movements of the headset and the two controllers. A user interacts with the VR environment using two controllers. Since the VR environment is presented at a room scale of approximately 6.5 feet by 5 feet, the presented environment is truly immersive, and a user can walk around and experience the scene the same way as in the real world.

There are many 3D modeling applications that have been developed for the HTC Vive and the Oculus Rift. Below is a list of some of those applications, along with the file types that each application supports for import and export. STL and OBJ are standard file formats for 3D printing. A 3D model created in a VR environment can be sent to a 3D printer once it is exported as an .stl or .obj file.

- MakeVR Pro is available for the HTC Vive and supports .sab, .sat, and .stl (import) and .sab, .stl, and .obj (export).[14]
- Medium runs on the Oculus Rift and the Samsung Gear, which uses the Samsung Galaxy smartphone. It supports .obj and .fbx (import) and .obj (export).[15]
- ShapeLab is available for both the HTC Vive and the Oculus Rift and supports .stl and .obj (import and export).[16]

- MasterpieceVR is available for both the HTC Vive and the Oculus Rift and supports .obj, .fbx, and .stl (import and export).[17]
- Gravity Sketch Pro is available for both the HTC Vive and the Oculus Rift, and the basic version supports .obj (import and export).[18]
- Google Blocks runs on both the HTC Vive and the Oculus Rift and supports .obj (export).[19]

In the next section, I will describe how a VR 3D modeling app works in comparison to a typical non-VR (meaning two-dimensional) 3D modeling application, using MakeVR Pro and Tinkercad as examples. MakeVR Pro, which runs on the HTC Vive, is a virtual reality 3D modeling app, while Tinkercad is a traditional two-dimensional 3D modeling application that runs on a web browser.

MAKEVR PRO VS. TINKERCAD

MakeVR Pro is built with a full CAD engine that has been optimized for 3D solid modeling, and it works well for designing an object for 3D printing. One starts MakeVR Pro by launching the application on the computer connected to the HTC Vive headset and the two sensors. The MakeVR Pro app can be purchased in Steam, an online game distribution platform.[20] The Pro version of MakeVR is recommended because it supports the .stl file import and export and includes precision 3D modeling tools.[21]

Navigation and Scaling

The way one typically examines a 3D object on a two-dimensional screen is by moving the object or the stage on which the object is located in order to view the object from different angles. In Tinkercad on a Mac (see figure 3.2), for example, a user can move around the stage by clicking the trackpad and dragging two fingers around. There are also buttons to click for zooming in and out as well as moving right, left, up, and down the stage.[22] In order to move an object, one uses a mouse or the arrow keys on the keyboard. Since the computer screen is two-dimensional and the object is three-dimensional, things can become a bit tricky. For example, to move an object up or down on the z axis, one needs to click the arrow-shaped pointer on top of the object. To scale an object, one clicks and drags a square-shaped point located at the four corners of the object. To rotate it, there are three curved double arrows to click for each of the x, y, and z axes.

Handling a 3D object is much easier and a lot more intuitive in the VR environment. In MakeVR Pro, one points to an object with the controller and selects it by pressing the trigger on the right controller. Once the object is selected, one can move it in the same way one would do in the real world. In

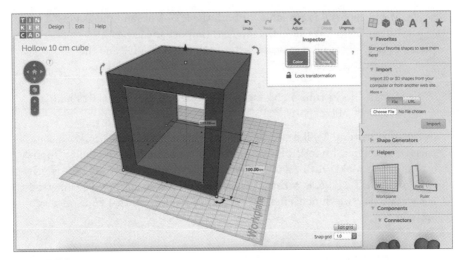

FIGURE 3.2
Tinkercad, a browser-based free 3D modeling software

order to scale the object, one presses the triggers on both controllers at the same time and makes an outward or inward gesture to increase or decrease the object's size. These gestures are intuitive enough that people can often figure them out by themselves without explicit instruction.

In the VR environment, one is not confined to looking at the modeled object from the outside. Instead, one is located in the same 3D world where an object is. Therefore, it is possible to scale an object to its real-life size and examine it as one would in the real world. The room-scale VR environment makes it easy for one to place multiple objects in different areas and put them together or take them apart without being restricted by the size of a computer screen. One can also build a whole scene that consists of multiple objects, and then walk through the scene. This can make a huge difference when designing a large structure like a building or a bridge. This kind of immersive experience is not something a traditional 2D-screen-based 3D modeling application like Tinkercad can provide.

Basic Tools

MakeVR Pro offers thirteen tools: Subtract, Add, Slice, Copy, Delete, Track, Move Pivot, Color & Texture, Sweep, Make Wire, Scale, Imprint, and Mirror. In order to access these tools, first bring out the menu tablet by pressing the small menu button on the left controller. Then select the "Tools" option by pressing the trigger button on the right controller (see figure 3.3).

Suppose one wants to create a window in a wall. One can do this by using subtraction. First, bring up a basic block and make it in the shape of a wall. Get another block and make it the size of a window. In MakeVR Pro, one would then choose the "Subtract" tool on the menu, select and bring the window

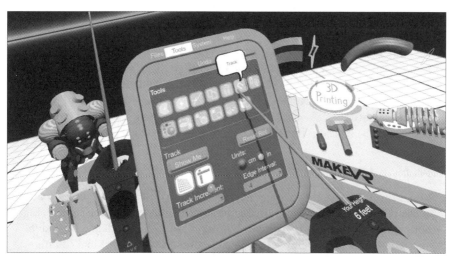

FIGURE 3.3
The "Tools" section on the MakeVR Pro menu

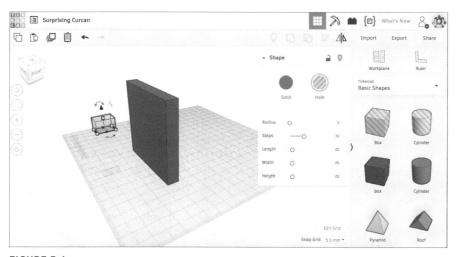

FIGURE 3.4
A solid wall and a hollow cube to be combined and
merged to create a window in Tinkercad

block to the wall in the desired position, and press the big round "Go" button
on the controller. This will subtract the part of the wall that came to overlap
with the window block from the wall, thereby creating a window in that place.

In Tinkercad, subtraction is done with a tool called "hole." Using the
same example above, one will set the type of the window-shaped block to
"hole" instead of "solid," position the window-shaped "hole" through the
wall as shown in figure 3.4, and then click the "Group" icon on the menu. The

wall-shaped hole and the wall will now have been merged, leaving a window in place.

The "Add" tool merges two objects that overlap with each other. In MakeVR Pro, this is called "addition." In Tinkercad, it is called "grouping." The "Add" operation in MakeVR Pro duplicates and adds the duplicated object. There is no such duplication in Tinkercad. "Slice" is only available in MakeVR Pro. The difference between "Slice" and "Subtract" is that when one uses "Slice," the part that is being sliced remains in place instead of being removed.

Precision Tools

While the VR environment may not make much difference in addition and subtraction, it certainly does in aligning multiple objects. Precisely aligning objects is a challenging but often necessary task in 3D modeling. It is difficult to get a good view of a 3D model object on a two-dimensional computer screen, and it is even more difficult when the object has a complicated structure. In a traditional 3D modeling application, two objects can appear to be adjacent to or touching each other from one angle when in reality they are far away from each other. This can only be discovered by viewing those objects from many different angles. For this reason, many users experience difficulties with aligning multiple 3D objects in a precise manner. It is also common to accidentally change the size or the shape of an object while trying to move the object.

Suppose that one wants to place a robot on a podium. For this, the robot must be placed exactly on the surface of the podium, not floating on top of it or partially buried into it, and ideally, it should be placed in the center. It is not difficult to bring the two objects close enough to overlap with each other. But placing one exactly on the surface of the other, thereby making the distance between the two objects zero, is not at all a trivial task in a traditional 3D modeling application.

To help with this type of precise alignment, Tinkercad provides what is called a "workplane." When one starts Tinkercad, one default workplane is already provided, and more can be brought out for alignment purposes. In order to place a robot on a podium, for example, one would first place a new workplane on top of the podium. Then, by moving the robot close to the workplane, one can make the robot snap onto that workplane. Once this is completed, the workplane between the podium and the robot can be removed. This works well on a flat surface. But for a curved surface, one must use multiple workplanes to accommodate the surface at different angles, and things can become complicated and frustrating.

By contrast, the "Track" and the "Move Pivot" tool in MakeVR Pro make the precise alignment of objects easy to perform. To use the same example above, select the robot, and choose the "Track" tool. Move the robot towards the podium. The robot will start tracking the surface of the podium. Note that the tracking will take place at the pivot point of the selected object. For this reason, if the pivot of the robot is in the center of its body, then the robot's center will track the top surface of a podium, and the robot will appear half submerged in the podium. The "Move Pivot" pool is used to change the pivot point. Once the robot's pivot point is moved to the center bottom, the robot's feet will track the surface of the podium.

A grid and a ruler are additional precision tools in Make VR Pro. A grid in MakeVR Pro is similar to a workplane in Tinkercad but is more versatile (see figure 3.5). It does not require a surface of an object to snap onto like a workplane in Tinkercad, and it can be used as a freestanding plane to arrange, reorient, and scale objects in precise positions. A ruler and a grid can be used separately or together to create a jig, a device used to maintain the correct positional relationship between parts of work during assembly, as shown in figure 3.6. The ruler and the grid are both scalable, and their unit of measurement can be changed between the metric and the imperial system. It is also possible to adjust the increment. The grid and the ruler in MakeVR Pro make it possible to place or connect multiple objects precisely where one would like them.

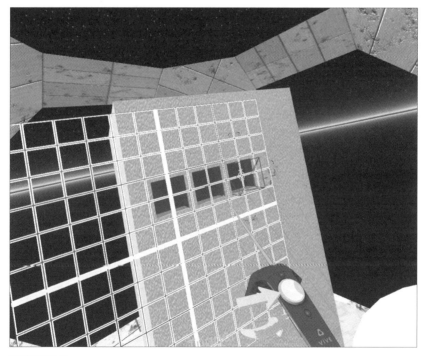

FIGURE 3.5

Window-sized holes created in MakeVR Pro using a grid attached on the wall. Compare this with figure 3.4.

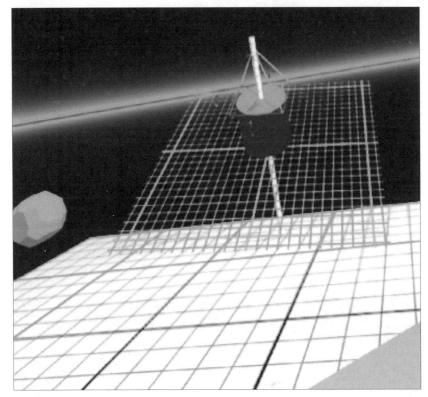

FIGURE 3.6.
An example of a grid and a ruler used as a jig in MakeVR Pro

Both MakeVR Pro and Tinkercad provide a radial snap grid that enables a user to rotate an object in an accurate angle on the x, y, and z axis as shown in figure 3.4. When the gesture in MakeVR Pro or the mouse movement in Tinkercad is made within the radial grid, an object pivots in angles of the scale on the grid. When the gesture or the mouse movement is made outside of the grid, one can pivot an object freely. Another tool that comes in handy for precision 3D modeling is the "Mirror" tool. This tool allows one to quickly create a part that precisely mirrors another part that has already been created. Both Tinkercad and MakeVR Pro provide the mirroring option.

Other Tools

There are several other tools available in MakeVR Pro and Tinkercad. Both MakeVR Pro and Tinkercad allow coloring an object, and MakeVR Pro has an additional texture option. Although texture is not something that is handled by a 3D printer, and the color of a model ultimately depends on the filament used in 3D printing, these options are no doubt fun to play around with.

Both MakeVR Pro and Tinkercad provide several premade objects such as blocks, cones, cylinders, spheres, pyramids, and so on. In MakeVR Pro, these "Primitives" are accessible from the "Files" menu. In Tinkercad, these are shown under "Basic Shapes" on the right-hand side of the screen. Tinkercad also provides additional objects under the categories of "Text and Numbers," "Characters," and "Connectors." On the other hand, MakeVR Pro enables a user to create a free-form object with the "Make Wire" and the "Sweep" tool, which are not available in Tinkercad.

Each tool in MakeVR Pro comes with a short "Show Me" tutorial. MakeVR Pro also contains a set of tutorials: Introduction, Navigation, Subtraction, Tools, Toolbox, Tracking, and Jigs. It is recommended that one should go through these tutorials before starting to build objects in MakeVR Pro. The same applies to Tinkercad, which provides many step-by-step lessons and tutorials.[23]

While there is some overlap in the tools that Tinkercad and MakeVR Pro offer, the VR environment of MakeVR Pro makes many 3D modeling tasks, particularly those that are tricky on a two-dimensional computer screen, more intuitive and easier to perform. This is indeed the greatest strength that the VR environment brings to a 3D modeling application. The more intuitive that 3D modeling operations are to perform, the faster people will be on their way to creating a 3D model instead of spending time on learning how to perform basic operations such as rotation, addition, and subtraction.

PRACTICAL CONSIDERATIONS FOR INTEGRATING VIRTUAL REALITY INTO A MAKERSPACE

A library with a preexisting makerspace is likely to find adding VR to the makerspace attractive.[24] In this chapter, I focused on a high-end VR system, the HTC Vive, and how MakeVR Pro, which runs on the HTC Vive, compares with a traditional two-dimensional 3D modeling application, Tinkercad, which runs on a web browser. A high-end VR system is required to run a sophisticated VR 3D modeling app and is also a good choice for a library makerspace because library patrons are less likely to own one at home. But there are many more affordable VR solutions if the goal is simply to offer some VR experience. For example, a Google Cardboard-type VR viewer costs as little as ten dollars and can turn a library user's smartphone into a VR device on the spot.[25] The Samsung Gear VR and the iPad Mini fitted in a large viewer can also be used for VR experience at a much lower price point.[26]

In terms of space planning, one needs some clear space in a room for a user to move around and explore the VR environment freely. The HTC Vive and the Oculus Rift can be set up to provide a room-scale VR environment of approximately 6.5 × 5 feet. A class or a small group of users are likely to congregate around the new VR system to see what the experience is like. For this reason, libraries should allow extra room to accommodate observers in their

FIGURE 3.7

An example VR space located inside the Makerspace
at the University of Rhode Island Libraries

VR space, and they should invest in an additional large-screen display that mirrors the screen of the computer connected to the VR system (see figure 3.7 for an example). This allows observers to watch what the person using the VR system sees at the same time. Another small but important thing to consider in the VR space planning is how to signify the VR area to a user wearing a headset, in order to prevent the user from moving out of the VR zone by accident, or bumping into the wall or the furniture. Placing a thick mat on the floor to cover the VR zone may be one solution. It will physically signal to the user if she steps out of the area. A separate room designated for VR experience may solve this problem and help with noise reduction at the same time.

If a library does not have a makerspace yet, then creating a VR space or a makerspace with VR as a strong component is an option.[27] 3D modeling is a lot more intuitive to learn and practice in the VR environment. For this reason, VR provides a great way to lead library patrons with little experience to 3D content creation. Integrating VR, particularly 3D modeling applications developed for the VR environment, into a new makerspace goes a long way towards growing more makers, which is the ultimate goal of a makerspace.

Including VR as a topic for makerspace events, workshops, and other programs can also maximize the benefit of a library makerspace. If a library makerspace already offers 3D printing, 3D scanning, or 3D modeling classes, adding the VR component to those classes would exemplify how the VR technology can be used for practical purposes. When a new technology is showcased at a library, the question of how it relates to existing library services often comes up. Addressing this kind of question can help people see the potential of a new technology and how it can be used for their benefit. For example, art students and instructors may find it fascinating to learn about the recent VR art exhibit, *The Enemy*, created by the Belgian-Tunisian photojournalist Karim Ben Khelifa. This 3,000-square-foot exhibit allowed up to fifteen museum visitors to walk around wearing the Oculus VR headset and experience what it is like to hear from a child soldier and a sergeant engaged in a war between Congo and Rwanda. These virtual characters directly speak to a museum visitor who is looking into their eyes in the VR exhibit.[28] Some library patrons may ask how VR is applicable to education. Children exploring mathematics, geography, or physics in the VR environment using ZSpace, one of the VR systems in the market, can provide a good example for these people.[29] Similarly, one can point to the NIH 3D Print Exchange (https://3dprint .nih.gov/) as a good case that demonstrates how 3D modeling and 3D printing are driving innovation in life sciences research and healthcare practices.

It is critical to involve library patrons and staff members in thinking about how a new technology such as VR can apply to their own areas of interest. This not only enables them to draw the connection between their interests and the new technology, but also serves as an effective way for a library to discover further avenues for future programs and partnership. Once those avenues are explored, the result can be compiled and presented as a set of compelling use cases that illustrate the value of VR or any other new technology offered by a library.[30]

NOTES

1. "Oculus Rift," https://www.oculus.com/rift; "VIVE," https://www.vive .com/us/.
2. For information about conversational interfaces, see Will Knight, "10 Breakthrough Technologies 2016: Conversational Interfaces," *MITechnology Review*, 2016, https://www.technologyreview.com/s/600766/ 10-breakthrough-technologies-2016-conversational-interfaces/.
3. Kasey Panetta, "Gartner Top 10 Strategic Technology Trends for 2018," Gartner, October 3, 2017, https://www.gartner.com/smarterwithgartner/ gartner-top-10-strategic-technology-trends-for-2018/.
4. "Tech Trends 2018: The Symphonic Enterprise," Deloitte Insights, https:// documents.deloitte.com/insights/TechTrends2018.
5. Mike Senese, "NASA Shapes the Future of Space Design and Exploration with Its Mixed Reality Program," Make, July 19, 2016, https://makezine .com/2016/07/19/rockets-rovers-mixed-reality/.
6. "Scopis," https://navigation.scopis.com/.

7. Microsoft, "Microsoft HoloLens," Microsoft HoloLens, https://www
.microsoft.com/en-us/hololens; Parker Wilhelm, "Microsoft HoloLens
Might One Day Assist in Spine Surgeries," TechRadar, May 5, 2017, https://
www.techradar.com/news/microsoft-hololens-could-one-day-assist-in
-spine-surgeries.

8. See Sophie Morlin-Yron, "Students Swim with Sharks, Explore Space,
through VR," CNN, September 19, 2017, https://www.cnn.com/2017/09/18/
health/virtual-reality-schools/index.html; and Jiabei Lei, "Adventures
Abound: Explore Google Expeditions on Your Own," *Google AR and VR* (blog),
July 19, 2017, https://www.blog.google/products/google-vr/adventures
-abound-explore-google-expeditions-your-own/. For Google Expeditions and
DiscoveryVR, see "Expeditions," Google Play, https://play.google.com/store/
apps/details?id=com.google.vr.expeditions; and "DiscoveryVR Education,"
Discovery Education UK, www.discoveryeducation.co.uk/discoveryvr.

9. For the explanation of a mesh, see "What Is a Mesh?" Blender 3D: Noob
to Pro, https://en.wikibooks.org/wiki/Blender_3D:_Noob_to_Pro/What
_is_a_Mesh%3F.

10. For common mesh errors in 3D printing, see "Fixing Non-Manifold Models,"
Shapeways, https://www.shapeways.com/tutorials/fixing-non-manifold
-models; and Sean Charlesworth, "Bits to Atoms: 3D Modeling Best Practices
for 3D Printing," Tested, March 19, 2014, www.tested.com/tech/3d
-printing/460456-bits-atoms-3d-modeling-best-practices-3d-printing/.

11. "Blender," https://www.blender.org/; "Rhino," https://www.rhin03d
.com/; "SketchUp," https://www.sketchup.com/home; "Solidworks," www
.solidworks.com/; "Tinkercad," https://www.tinkercad.com/.

12. Bohyun Kim and Brian Zelip, "Growing Makers in Medicine, Life Sciences,
and Healthcare" (presentation, Association of College & Research Libraries
Conference, Baltimore, MD, March 24, 2017), https://www.slideshare.net/
bohyunkim/growing-makers-in-medicine-life-sciences-and-healthcare.

13. The difference between a 3D modeling and a sculpting tool lies in whether
the application treats a 3D object as a mesh or a model. A "mesh" of a
3D object is a digital representation of its shape that consists of a set
number of polygons, while a "model" of a 3D object means a mathematical
representation of the object in terms of the NURBS (nonuniform rational
basis spline) surfaces. CAD software generates a 3D model with NURBS
surfaces, which is solid. In contrast, a mesh may not have a valid real-
world 3D geometry to be a solid object, although it may look like it. What
this means is that a sculpting tool will generate 3D objects that cannot be
3D-printed, while a 3D modeling application will always generate a solid,
watertight object that can be 3D-printed without a mesh error.

14. "MakeVR Pro," Vive, https://www.viveport.com/apps/9e94a10f-51d9
-4b6f-92e4-6e4fe9383fe9.

15. "Medium," Oculus, https://www.oculus.com/medium/.

16. "ShapeLab," https://info.leopoly.com/shapelab.

17. "MasterpieceVR—FAQ," https://www.masterpiecevr.com/faq.

18. "Gravity Sketch VR," http://store.steampowered.com/app/551370/Gravity
    _Sketch_VR/.

19. "Blocks," https://vr.google.com/blocks/.

20. MakeVR Pro can be purchased at http://store.steampowered.com/app/
    569180/MakeVR_Pro/. MakeVR is available for free at https://www.viveport
    .com/apps/23d40515–641c-4adb-94f5–9ba0ed3deed5 and lacks several
    features of MakeVR Pro.

21. An imported 3D model in .stl file format can be scaled and moved around in
    MakeVR Pro, but it cannot be modified or saved.

22. These controls received a slight change in the Tinkercad beta version. The
    arrow buttons moving the angle right, left, up, and down were removed in
    the beta version. See figure 3.2 for the current version of Tinkercad. See
    figure 3.4 for the beta version of Tinkercad.

23. "Learn," Tinkercad, https://www.tinkercad.com/learn/.

24. For examples, see Miguel Figueroa, "In a Virtual World: How School,
    Academic, and Public Libraries Are Testing Virtual Reality in Their
    Communities," *American Libraries* 49, no. 3/4 (April 3, 2018): 26–33.

25. "Google Cardboard," https://vr.google.com/cardboard/.

26. For a detailed rundown of VR systems and headsets by their price range
    and capabilities, see David Greene and Michael Groenendyk, "Virtual and
    Augmented Reality as Library Services," *Computers in Libraries* 38, no. 1
    (February 1, 2018): 4–7.

27. An example of a recent makerspace with the VR component embedded is
    at the Ralph W. Steen Library, Stephen F. Austin University in Texas. Their
    VR-based makerspace opened in 2016. For their approach, see Edward
    Iglesias, "Creating a Virtual Reality-Based Makerspace," *Online Searcher* 42,
    no. 1 (February 1, 2018): 36–39.

28. Wade Roush, "This VR Exhibit Lets You Connect with the Human Side of
    War," *MIT Technology Review,* December 6, 2017, https://www.technology
    review.com/s/609316/this-vr-exhibit-lets-you-connect-with-the-human-side
    -of-war/.

29. "Force: Acceleration and Velocity," zSpace, https://zspace.com/edu/content/
    subjects/mathematics/functions/4061. For more examples of VR being used
    for different subjects, see https://zspace.com/edu/content.

30. Compelling use cases for a makerspace can be collected and distributed in
    the form of a newsletter. See the example of the online newsletter archive
    of the University of Maryland Baltimore, Health Sciences and Human
    Services Library's Innovation Space at https://us5.campaign-archive.com/
    home/?u=8d6a2c0e62ab4cc63311ab6cd&id=7b7755271d.

BRANDON PATTERSON, TALLIE CASUCCI,
THOMAS FERRILL, and GREG HATCH

4

Play, Education, and Research

Exploring Virtual Reality through Libraries

AS CAMPUS DEMAND AND INTEREST IN VIRTUAL REALITY EXPANDS, so does the need to increase access to this technology. Academic libraries, as interdisciplinary spaces for collaboration and connection, play an important role in sharing emerging technologies with their communities. Discoverability through games, models for learning, and connecting researchers to resources are all ways that libraries use play, education, and research as pillars for scholarly success. In this chapter, two libraries at the University of Utah explore the concepts of play, education, and research using VR and envision the future success of the technology.

THE BEGINNINGS OF VIRTUAL REALITY AT THE UNIVERSITY OF UTAH

From 3D renderings of vehicles in training simulation systems to watching your favorite character in the latest computer-animated movie, much of the technology used to develop such visuals came from the research of talented faculty members at the University of Utah. The computer graphics industry began in the 1970s with two Utah computer science faculty members, David

Evans and Ivan Sutherland, who developed some of the first VR simulation systems, which were initially used by the U.S. military. As early as 1965, Sutherland imagined VR technology as a wholly immersive experience and illuminated its future uses:

> The ultimate display would, of course, be a room within which the computer can control the existence of matter. A chair displayed in such a room would be good enough to sit in. Handcuffs displayed in such a room would be confining, and a bullet displayed in such a room would be fatal. With appropriate programming such a display could literally be the Wonderland into which Alice walked.[1]

In the era of Evans and Sutherland, graduates of the university's computer science program made seminal contributions to rendering, shading, animation, visualization, and what would eventually be known as virtual reality, notably in the work of John Warnock, Ed Catmull, Henri Gouraud, Bui Tuong Phong, Fred Parke, Jim Kajiya, and others.[2] These pioneers oversaw the emergence of 3D raster graphics research, much of it government-funded.[3] The University of Utah became the world's preeminent center for computer graphics research, with graduates launching Netscape, Adobe, and Pixar.[4] These technologies also helped to create a display for 3D data, with optical tracking for interactions between viewers or performers and the visualizations. This made possible VR experiences in art and entertainment, such as Ellen Bromberg's screendance experiments[5] and Another Language Performing Arts Company's real-time, distributed, and surrealistic cinema.[6]

THE LIBRARIES' ADOPTION OF VIRTUAL REALITY

The Spencer S. Eccles Health Sciences Library (Eccles) and the J. Willard Marriott Library (Marriott), both at the University of Utah, have strong interests in virtual reality. Both libraries are influenced by novel research and educational activities around campus, as well as high-grade and low-cost consumer market technology. Eccles and Marriott report to different campus administrators, operate on separate budgets, and have independent mission statements and strategic plans. At the same time, their library personnel collaborate closely to create a centralized library catalog, provide access to a core collection of research databases, and share physical resources through intercampus document delivery and high-density storage. Both libraries have frequently been early adopters of new technology, have made strategic hires of both faculty and staff to develop technology-rich resources and services, and continue to invest in equipment to better serve their communities. Each library has VR systems that are part of a larger pool of "interactive media" offerings, broadly defined to include a spectrum of augmented, virtual, and mixed reality, as well as console and handheld video gaming systems. The available software includes games, apps, experimental simulations, and learning software. In addition, the libraries deploy interactive media hardware in designated areas and make it available for checkout.

Eccles serves University of Utah Health, which encompasses both academic and clinical services in the health sciences. The library's mission is to "advance and transform education, research, and health care through dynamic technologies, evidence application, and collaborative partnerships." To help achieve this mission, two librarians were hired to focus on technologies and innovative strategies in order to build an infrastructure that supports tools like VR interaction. Eccles partners with faculty, staff, and students from the five Health Sciences schools and colleges (Dentistry, Health, Medicine, Nursing, and Pharmacy) to consider investing in worthwhile emerging technologies. As VR continues to gain traction within the health sciences community, especially as a tool for simulating real-life scenarios in medical care, the librarians build connections with those outside the health sciences community in order to further knowledge of the subject. Great insights into the potential benefits of VR come from collaborations with faculty in the Entertainment Arts & Engineering (EAE) program. As experts in the field of virtual environments, EAE faculty build interdisciplinary teams of engineers, artists, and producers that have attracted Health Sciences researchers' attention. Additionally, VR is one of the primary initiatives of an academic integration working group that is focusing on educational technologies in the health sciences, further incentivizing the need to explore the technology.

In 2017, Eccles secured funding for VR equipment with a regional Technology Improvement Award from the National Network of Libraries of Medicine, MidContinental Region. The grant allowed the library to create a VR space with an Oculus Rift headset, controllers, sensors, desktops, and several commercial VR games. The VR space enabled the exploration of library collections in new ways. A partnership between Eccles and Neuro-Ophthalmology was expanded to use VR as a means to visualize a virtual neuroanatomy library.[7] Future funding for VR equipment to support the neuroanatomy project and others will likely come from internal funds, such as the library's Student Computing Fee fund or university grant funding. In addition to VR, Eccles has invested in 3D printing/fabrication, virtual anatomy, and multimedia presentation equipment and software to assist health sciences researchers and educators.

The Marriott is located in the heart of the campus and serves students and faculty from colleges and schools in the arts, humanities, social sciences, sciences, engineering, business, and architecture. The library began experimenting with interactive media, Second Life, in 2008. The library built on earlier successes in media-editing equipment and wide-format printing, and library patrons continued to express interest in new types of technology, such as 3D modeling, scanning, and printing equipment, which were first purchased in

2011. A wave of inexpensive 3D printer technology allowed projects, championed by library personnel, to turn into full-fledged operations serving all of the campus.

In spring 2016, the Marriott began purchasing interactive media using funds allocated from the arts and humanities collection development budget. Interactive media were purchased on the premise that video games and gaming systems are the equivalent of books for the EAE program's faculty and students, fulfilling one of the library's strategic directions to "creatively use resources . . . to meet campus needs." The EAE liaisons promoted the newly available interactive media resources to students and encouraged faculty members to incorporate the resources into their curricula. Anticipating pushback from some library employees about the value of interactive media and the perception that they are simply for entertainment, the liaisons presented at all-staff meetings, articulating interactive media's alignment with the university's and Marriott's missions, and they invited public service staff to refer inquiries back to the liaisons. Documentation of high circulation rates of games and gaming systems within the first six months helped to secure additional, ongoing funding.

Also in spring 2016, Marriott purchased a Microsoft HoloLens using library-allocated Student Computing Fee funds. The Marriott's library dean received a demonstration of that piece of early, consumer-grade VR equipment. Her interest in it was compounded by a business trip to North Carolina State University, where she experienced the new, technology-rich Hunt Library. In summer 2016, she invited the library's EAE liaisons to compile a wish list of additional interactive media equipment, and she ultimately approved nearly $8,000 for new VR equipment, including HTC Vive and Oculus Rift gaming systems, and two VR-ready laptop computers. Continued funding for the technology has been secured by documenting successful and impactful uses of VR equipment. The initial investments in interactive media equipment were enhanced by the creation of a unit of Marriott staff dedicated to this purpose. Altogether, this service model has enabled researchers and students to approach existing problems with new resources and expertise.

Video games and gaming systems were immediately deployed and circulated in easy-to-access areas in close proximity to Marriott's Knowledge Commons computer lab. This barrier-free deployment was extended to 3D printing equipment in spring 2017, and to VR systems in fall 2017. Recognizing that VR encompasses a whole host of platforms and history, five service models have evolved in both libraries:

- Open lab space: for walk-in use
- Closed lab space: for demonstrations, testing, and staging new equipment releases
- Flexible lab space: reservable, for class or team use (currently in planning phase)
- Checkout equipment: for individual use

- VR developer kits (laptop and VR equipment): for checkout, to use for research, demonstrations, and presentations outside of the library

VIRTUAL REALITY AS PLAY

Libraries are in a position to offer space and host events that provide access for community members to play in VR while accompanied by staff support and resources. When pairing a display of someone playing in VR with an intellectually curious crowd, sparks of invention and possibility come to the minds of those watching, intriguing them to take part in the action. The Marriott and Eccles libraries serve as spaces where students are already interacting with technology on a daily basis, so the setup to encounter and use VR systems is compatible with existing technology services and workflows. As of June 2018, students visiting the Marriott's Knowledge Commons can log in and launch software for two Oculus Rifts and an HTC Vive system. Students can also check out an HTC Vive, Oculus Rift, or Microsoft HoloLens for presentations, development, and research studies in their own rooms, labs, or work spaces. By lowering the barriers to entry, more students and faculty become interested in ways that VR can change their learning environment. Early circulation statistics suggest significant growth in demand for this equipment. In the first nine months of deployment, VR peripherals and equipment had 560 circulations. Early outreach efforts, such as workshops and weekly demonstrations, have evolved into permanent VR development spaces, consultation services, and several long-term interdisciplinary projects in medicine, architecture, art, geography, and engineering. What started as a casual exploration of VR soon became a serious endeavor to assist researchers with the adoption of VR technology in a variety of fields.

The willingness to play creates a gateway to engagement and invites users from all disciplines to experiment. In pursuit of this type of discovery, the Marriott has adopted a wide range of consumer VR hardware. Patrons can test the major VR platforms and peripherals by playing a wide variety of games and apps that are available. Peripherals, such as Vive Trackers for locating real-world objects in VR, and PSVR Aim, a controller for precise motion tracking, are simple to use and ease the point of entry for those new to VR. Staff from the Marriott continue to investigate ways to integrate other technology into the service model, including batteries and packs for untethered VR, motion capture suits for VR integration, Leap Motion for real-time hand and digit tracking, and a steering wheel and pedals for driving simulations. Having these available for demonstration and circulation allows a more robust experimentation capacity for diverse communities.

In 2012, the Libraries Innovation Team (LIT) was formed with the goal of connecting library resources in order to stimulate ideas and maintain services related to intellectual property and commercialization. LIT consists of a group of library personnel who are dedicated to the multiple innovative programs at the university. The team is a mobile unit that hosts drop-in, hands-on, and play-based sessions in the newly built Lassonde Studios, an entrepreneurial student co-living and co-working space connected to the David Eccles School of Business. Showcasing VR equipment has led to conversations about ideation, patent searches, and design. While students interact with VR, the LIT discusses library resources and services, often resulting in student consultations with librarians.

The creation of the LIT has led to the library's involvement in competitions in gaming using VR technology.[8] In 2014, the Games4Health student game design competition was created at the University of Utah. In 2017, a total of 160 college teams from 21 states, 86 universities, and 14 countries created games that impact health, under the auspices of this competition. The competition is focused on several challenges: corporate wellness, fitness, clinical health, chronic diseases, and adolescent mental well-being. Submissions include games that encourage exercise, meditation, adherence to prescribed medications, and other successful behavioral changes. University librarians, faculty, and staff serve as judges and vote on projects based on the game idea, consumer need, and business plan. The competition continues to grow in VR representation. From 2016 to 2017, VR submissions grew by 10 percent, making up 50 percent of total submissions. The growing number of students creating VR games during the competition reveals the growing interest in VR for health sciences applications. This competition suggests a strong link between play and health, and provided the impetus for the Eccles to secure grant funding for a VR space.

VIRTUAL REALITY AS EDUCATION

As patrons across campus gain exposure to VR, demand and interest in the educational possibilities of the technology continue to expand. Through library demonstrations in classes and public forums, faculty find ways to integrate the technology into their curricula. They often send students in small groups to explore VR in the library and write about their experience, as it pertains to their class topic. To better meet this need, Marriott and Eccles hired student developers for VR to complement other educational experiences happening in the library. A student developer is partnered with a campus faculty member to develop a game or application specific to their class, or to adapt an already existing game or application. VR developer kits are available for checkout, so faculty and students can develop their own projects at a self-guided pace.

Students investigate VR environments, play the latest content, and import their own designs. Examples from faculty who have integrated VR into their courses include:

- Architecture students explore their designs at "true" scale by importing site plans, building massings into virtual environments, and performing virtual walk-throughs.
- Geography students using the Google Earth app utilize VR to explore energy production sites around the world, gaining insights into the scope and impact of various types of energy production.
- Dental students use custom VR software to practice preparing fillings, explore patient case studies, and refine tool-handling techniques.
- Fine arts students explore various artistic mediums, including VR sculpting software.
- Nursing students use a VR Nursing Simulation Toolkit to practice patient scenarios and evaluate their performance.

Many of these projects originated from informal meetings between faculty and library personnel. A project with the School of Dentistry started from a weekly open house at the Marriott. In February 2017, members of LIT, including a student employee who had developed a simple VR application, gave a demonstration of the library's VR equipment to several Dentistry faculty members, including the dean of the School of Dentistry. He envisioned the student's work as a possible cost-saving solution for School of Dentistry training.

The student partnered with a Dentistry faculty member and they identified dental education training that could benefit from VR, developed workflows, and incorporated feedback from students and faculty. Within a few months, the VR software was incorporated into the preclinical and clinical curriculum for dental students. The procedures now learned in VR include measuring cavity and crown preparations using a VR depth gauge on 3D-scanned teeth, making crown and cavity preparations using a tracked dental drill, and visualizing cone beam CT scan data. Instructors can also compare student work with their own at a magnified scale using 3D-scanned tooth preparations. The VR software gives students hands-on experiences with workflows they will encounter regularly, and allows for a lower cost and better assessment of common procedures. This collaboration continues to blend the best of library services, student talent, faculty innovation, and a new wave of previously inaccessible technology.

Additionally, the Health Sciences schools and colleges have formed task forces to reenvision education to include emerging technologies. The workgroup includes representatives from Eccles and Marriott who have provided several proof-of-concept educational VR examples, including the newly developed Dentistry training tools. The grand vision of the emerging technologies work group is to create development hubs within both libraries. These hubs will continue to create VR educational experiences that can be embedded into curricula and classes.

VIRTUAL REALITY AS RESEARCH

Research with VR is the logical next step leading to increased educational uses and scholarly input. One major research group at the University of Utah leveraging VR is the *Therapeutic Games and Applications Laboratory*, or The GApp Lab. The GApp Lab was created to use games as research and education tools in the health sciences. It consists of about 35 graduate students, two staff, a faculty director, and numerous faculty collaborators. The students work in teams of three (artist, engineer, and producer) to develop various games and application projects. The GApp Lab is part of the Center for Medical Innovation, housed in Eccles, and a librarian assists with grant proposals to gain additional development funding, conducts literature searches, and advises on study designs and a data management plan.[9] A librarian also co-teaches a three-credit graduate EAE course, "Serious Games," a genre which explores health, education, military, and other games with a primary purpose other than entertainment.

Roger Altizer, director of The GApp Lab and digital medicine at the Center for Medical Innovation, explains why he believes The GApp Lab belongs in the library:

> Folks in health sciences, business, engineering, the arts, and professionals from the community all find the library to be a space to find and create new knowledge together. The library has always been a place where knowledge lived, now it has become a place where interdisciplinary teams innovate and technology thrives. More than a good host, the library is facilitating exciting work that will have a huge impact on the future of healthcare. The next wave of digital medicine has already started here in the library.[10]

Recent VR projects developed by The GApp Lab include Virtual Medical Records and ChoreograFish. Virtual Medical Record (https://youtu.be/nTB_Fg4vmc4) is a simulation for diabetic patients that imports the patient's glucose data from the electronic medical record into a VR setting. Patients can interact with their data in a more compelling visual manner. ChoreograFish (https://youtu.be/sshcJOxVZQQ) is an underwater VR game for children with autism to choreograph schools of fish. The project investigates spatial reasoning for children as they combine music and 3D fish movements. For both of these VR projects, librarians assisted with grant proposals to gain additional development funding and conduct literature searches, study design development, and data management. The GApp Lab and Eccles plan to fund current and future research endeavors through the financial support of additional research grant applications.

ENABLING FUTURE SUCCESS

When considering VR and the future of academic libraries, it is important to recognize VR as just the newest piece in an ever-evolving system. Library spaces have long been in fluctuation, with computer labs moving from general productivity to specialized equipment. The expertise of library personnel continues to expand beyond general reference in order to assist students and faculty who are looking to experiment with the latest technology. While the circulation of books and journals is on the decline, circulation is on the rise for media equipment, computers, and now, VR headsets. A library's willingness to investigate technology resources for students and the research community establishes it as a clearinghouse for new approaches to complex problems. As a shared resource, the library is a polestar for disparate fields to engage in dialogue and work collaboratively on projects.

Investing in new technology initiatives requires support from several organizational levels. At the top, the university and library administration should encourage the growth of new programming and back it with financing, which will give structural support to expand the uses of technology. At the middle level, managers and librarians should be involved to ensure an alignment with existing resource allocations, staff productivity, and institutional mission, in order to build successful relationships with those in the campus community. On the ground, professional and hourly library staff should be empowered to set up, experiment with, and present the technology to university faculty and students and to the broader community.

Additional consideration should be made regarding accessibility to resources, employee development, user training, repurposing space, and identifying services that meet patrons' stated and anticipated needs. As with many library services, these activities require input from within the library and throughout the campus and community; success is dependent upon the engagement and creative energy of many individuals. Through coordinated effort, projects that utilize VR and future technological advances will thrive in an academic library environment.

With the successful development of VR collaborations at the University of Utah, it is exciting to think of the future possibilities. The interconnectedness of Eccles, Marriott, and campus-wide stakeholders—and the collegial relationships of motivated individuals—has enabled teams to come together and establish forward momentum. With continued collaborative effort, VR has unlimited potential to further strengthen relationships, improve learning, and create new knowledge.

ACKNOWLEDGMENTS

Thank you to our colleagues who shared their insight and expertise to improve this chapter. We are also thankful to those who create, inspire, share, collaborate, and lead the way to explore emerging technologies that enhance our learning environment.

NOTES

1. Ivan E. Sutherland, "The Ultimate Display," in *Information Processing 1965: Proceedings of the International Federation of Information Processing Congress*, (Washington, DC: Spartan Books, 1965), 506–8.

2. Wayne E. Carlson, "Basic and Applied Research Moves in the Industry," in *Computer Graphics and Computer Animation: A Retrospective Overview* (Columbus: Ohio State University Press, 2017), chap. 4, 90–99, https:// ohiostate.pressbooks.pub/graphicshistory/.

3. Brad A. Myers, "A Brief History of Human-Computer Interaction Technology," *ACM interactions* 5, no. 2 (1998): 44–54.

4. Karen Paik, *To Infinity and Beyond! The Story of Pixar Animation Studios* (San Francisco: Chronicle Books, 2007), 12–27.

5. Erin Brannigan, *Dancefilm: Choreography and the Moving Image* (New York: Oxford University Press, 2011).

6. Elizabeth Ann Miklavcic and Jimmy Miklavcic, "Interplay: Performing on a High-Tech Wire (Collaborative, Real-Time, Distributed, Surrealistic Cinema)," (paper presented at the Utah Academy of Sciences, Arts, & Letters, 2007).

7. Nancy Lombardo, Kathleen B. Digre, and Larry Frohman. "Neuro-Ophthalmology Virtual Education Library (NOVEL: http://novel.utah .edu/)," *Journal of Neuro-Ophthalmology* 30, no. 3 (2010): 301–2, https://doi .org/10.1097/WNO.0b013e3181ebded8.

8. Erin Wimmer et al., "Medical Innovation Competition Information Support," in *Information and Innovation: A Natural Combination for Health Sciences Libraries* (Lanham, MD: Rowman & Littlefield, 2017), chap. 10, 99–116.

9. Tallie Casucci, "Information Needs of Medical Digital Therapeutics Personnel," in *Information and Innovation: A Natural Combination for Health Sciences Libraries* (Lanham, MD: Rowman & Littlefield, 2017), chap. 9, 89–98.

10. Roger Altizer Jr., "Library Champion," in *eSynapse—Eccles Health Sciences Library Newsletter* 29, no. 2 (Salt Lake City: University of Utah, 2014), 5–8, http://library.med.utah.edu/or/esynapse/2014-Vol29-No2.pdf.

5

Every Student Her Universe

Alternate Academic Realities

S. R. RANGANATHAN WAS ENDURINGLY CORRECT ABOUT SO *MUCH* when he set his restless mind to thinking about the library. Of *course* every one of its books is of interest to someone, hence we should ease that person's path to finding it. And each library ought to have at least a book or two suited to every type of person who drops in.

This is axiomatic. No room for dispute. Even if books as the great Madras librarian knew them are not the medium of the moment, disputing his laws of library science is as perverse as arguing against gravity, which tugs as sternly on a dropped iPhone X as it did on Newton's apple.

The organism that Ranganathan wrote about and served so generously *has* continued to grow in ways that are surely beyond the wildest fancies of the man who laid down its laws at the dawn of the 1930s. Few of the library's sometimes awkward growth spurts have been as embarrassing as our anguished debates around which types of media belong in its collection. Films? LPs? *Unheard of!* VHS tapes? The Internet? *Absurd!* E-books? Streaming video? *Unthinkable! This is a library! Liber, libri, librorum!*

Library builders of a century ago judged it worth the trouble and expense to chisel names of noted authors into granite; their assumption that MILTON and TENNYSON would mean something to literate onlookers throughout the life of a masonry structure must have seemed reasonable at the time. In 2018 on our public university campus in Pennsylvania, the former library building still sports those perplexing strings of stone-carved letters. And there is now, seemingly, a distinct notion of *Library* in the mind of every student. Any vestigial image of *the place with the books* is mere sentimental shorthand: our place incorporates tutoring and writing centers, computer labs and a café, vending machines and giant screens, plus a makerspace workroom, along with occasional massage and pet therapy. Clearly what magnetizes the library for many visitors is something other than its *books,* whose circulation perennially declines.

The strong, steady flow of new media platforms in this century has upended consumption habits while naturally eroding some once commonly understood cultural referents. A fix that is often applied to atomized collegians in the United States asks students to join in a "common read"[1] as part of their first-year experience. Mass immersion in a single book aims to build communal references that can help a professor connect with students whose tastes in reading, binge watching, web browsing, music and podcast listening, and perhaps most significantly, video gaming, might well have no overlap with the professor's own tastes.

Each incoming freshman class brings a panoply of new realities and in turn develops subtly disparate notions of what their library even *is.* What is more, libraries themselves have a complicated relationship with reality. Are they stolid repositories of vetted data and firm facts? Certainly, but so much *else* besides: save for some rigorously curated special collections, we are *all* teeming with fantastical speculation, stale propaganda, and fanciful stories with scarcely a toe in the tepid pond water of real life. While most *academic* libraries do not traffic as heavily in unhinged romance as the typical public library must, we nonetheless harbor countless alternate realities. The university library where I work? It proudly shelves the ravings of a mad Danish prince who never existed, utopian pipe dreams of a long-dead Greek political theorist, and more than a few sketchy tales about vampires.

In conversations with undergraduates about what libraries are and what *library-ness* includes, we are surprised anew every year. The conception and understanding of our library in the mind's eye of a member of the Class of 2022 can be wildly different from the library that occupies *my* head. It must be. His version of our building might even be a different color than mine, yet it is every bit as *real.*

So, what about virtual reality, then? Does that, and a collection of canonical VR games, merit a place in our stately and respectable academic library? How can there be any doubt?

INSTITUTIONAL OVERVIEW

Kutztown University (KU) is a member of the fourteen-campus Pennsylvania State System of Higher Education (PASSHE), which is *not* part of the Penn State University system. KU's rural campus (in Kutztown, PA) is surrounded by farmland, but two of the state's five most populous urban centers, Allentown and Reading, are a half-hour drive in either direction. KU is ninety minutes from Philadelphia and two hours from New York City. The Borough of Kutztown's population of 5,000 year-round residents swells appreciably during the fall and spring semesters: the university's FTE enrollment has stabilized near 8,500 in recent years. Founded in 1866, the school has long offered MA and MS degrees through its colleges of Education, Arts and Sciences, Business, and Visual and Performing Arts. In 2015 its first joint doctoral program was launched in partnership with another PASSHE school, and in 2017 KU introduced its own EdD program.

Originally the state's normal school, KU is well regarded regionally for its education programs, including a strong one for K–12 librarians. The university's unremarkable fall 2016 acceptance rate of 80 percent, with a mean high school GPA of 3.16, belies the fact that a handful of its degree tracks (notably in the visual arts) have stringent entrance requirements. KU is viewed locally as a solid working-class public university with relatively low tuition that draws many students from Philadelphia and New Jersey.

The campus library is a three-story building of 122,670 square feet. Our virtual reality facilities are remote from its sole entrance and other high-traffic areas, on the level below the main floor in a converted office that holds the library's makerspace, called STEAMworks; the acronym in its name, a play on STEM (science, technology, engineering, math), befits a school that offers no engineering degrees but boasts outstanding programs in art—the *A* in STEAM.

The 1,500-square-foot room that now houses the makerspace had lain fallow for several years as a storage unit for old equipment. But its physical configuration is unique in our fifty-year-old building: for much of the space's history it had been a work area for what was effectively the campus instructional technology operation. A decade on, there remained for the nascent makerspace an intact workbench, plus an array of shelving packed with tools and equipment ranging from wrenches and paintbrushes to working camcorders and soldering equipment.

The room was a natural spot for a makerspace, which was one of the priorities of our recently installed library director. The director's background in computer science made her perhaps unusually sympathetic to peculiar requests like the purchase of a cutting-edge VR headset plus a powerful gaming PC to run it, along with a line in the library's acquisitions budget.[2]

DESCRIPTION OF THE TECHNOLOGY

Our flagship virtual reality rig is the HTC Vive. When installed in August 2016, it was the only publicly available VR setup in PASSHE, and the Vive was the consumer market's only *room-scale* VR system. This term bears explanation.

Room-scale VR technology tracks and precisely registers the user's actual position in physical space, enabling well-written interactive software to respond accordingly to movement. Imagine goggles encasing your eyes, show-ing—in virtual reality—framed paintings hanging on the far wall of a room, apparently a few paces away. Each step or roll forward using your *real* legs or chair brings the paintings closer in your perception. As you near the virtual wall, reaching with your real hand that holds a tracking device enables you to grab a VR brochure beside the now-nearby painting. Turning your head a few degrees to the left brings a neighboring painting into focus; you can sidle up beside it, or perhaps turn your body 180 degrees to see from a distance the sculpture that was beside you when your journey began.

Vive hardware comprises a headset, a pair of handheld controllers, and two "lighthouses," black base stations slightly larger than a Rubik's cube that define a calibrated "play area" according to their positions at opposite corners of a rectangle spanning at most about 16.5 feet between the units—in our case a square with 12-foot sides.

The lighthouses emit timed infrared pulses, sweeping the play area with invisible light from lasers and LEDs. Motors running silently at 3,600 RPM drive these emissions, while the Vive headset and handheld controllers sense the light from the base stations, enabling the CPU to calculate the real-time positions and orientations of the user's head and hands.[3]

Two lenses inside the sealed headset are the wearer's only sources of visual information. A forward-facing camera in the headset's exterior enables the user to optionally and situationally see the outlines of nearby objects and people. This feature activates when the player crosses the play area's bound-aries: depending on the system settings, she might first see a virtual "cage" defined by laser-like beams of light, beyond which the edges and outlines of her surroundings are apparent. The headset, outfitted with an earphone jack and an onboard microphone, is tethered to the CPU by two long HDMI and USB cables. The player's view is typically mirrored, albeit in 2D, on a monitor or a large screen.

The handheld controllers are outfitted with a large four-way trackpad but-ton, two side grip buttons, and a trigger. In use, they are perhaps reminiscent of the batons waved near airport runways, except that the Vive controller's most remarkable function lies in its *reception* of light from the twin base sta-tions. The controllers are proxies for hands, for claws, or for tools; depending on a game's design, players might use one or both of them to grab, hold, swat, or throw VR objects. In many contexts they can also trigger menu choices, shoot lasers, or "teleport" the user: in the museum example above, you might have saved time, and a few steps, by pointing a controller to the other side of the room.

This HTC hardware has been fairly simple to maintain and reliably trouble-free. A controller that failed us early on was quickly replaced at no charge. We paid $800 in 2016 for the system: two lighthouses, two controllers, a headset, some cabling, and a junction box (its price by early 2018 had fallen to $500). The more expensive part of our virtual reality setup cost us more than half again as much: a Dell XPS 8900 Special Edition (i.e., VR-ready) desktop computer with an NVIDIA GTX 970 graphics card. This was at the time perhaps the least expensive ready-made computer capable of running Vive VR. Though reviews in major online forums suggested that it might be underpowered for the purpose, we have not had issues with "lag" (latency), nor have we heard complaints from our local gaming cognoscenti.

Gaming PCs are not routine purchases for many libraries. When considering what hardware to get, it makes sense to consult with avid gamers on your library's staff and in its tech support shop—you can be sure there are several—and in your user community. Their expertise is invaluable, even if the reliability of their opinions is sometimes clouded by tribal passions.[4]

WHY WE SELECTED THE HTC VIVE

Our library's makerspace struggled with its identity from the beginning. The project's initial charge was open-ended; some viewed it as a lab, a clearinghouse for unspecified "emerging technologies." STEAMworks opened in February 2016, a half-year before we got the Vive. In addition to a makeshift video production area, some low-end 3D printers, a vinyl cutter, and a button machine, we had a primitive VR device, Google Cardboard, given to us at closing time of a World Maker Faire in New York. It requires the insertion of a smartphone with stereoscopic apps that rely on the phone's accelerometer, magnetometer, and gyroscope to interactively respond to motions of the user's head.

These simple goggles attracted enough interest to suggest that a more ambitious version of such experiences could be popular in our space. Observing Google Cardboard in use revealed an intriguing aspect of VR play: while deeply immersive for the participant, half the fun goes to bystanders laughing at their masked peer's antics while relentlessly sharing them on social media. We saw VR experiences catalyze friendly interaction between players and their fascinated audiences.

Perceptive students in the campus computer science club pitched the Vive to us in winter 2016, amid the early buzz ahead of its April release. VR was an easy sell. I had recently experienced an impressive training simulation run by a trade school: donning a welding mask that was actually a VR headset, I found myself straddling a steel girder high atop a bridge under construction. Battling vertigo, I laid down a bead while sparks flew and I tried to ignore the river far below. When I finished, the software graded the quality of my work, giving me a score. This felt like the future of learning.

We deliberated before choosing the Vive. Oculus was commanding most of the media's attention (this groundbreaking brand remains a popular synecdoche for consumer VR itself), but it was still a stationary experience. HTC's room-scale system represented an advance that would take VR well beyond seated roller-coaster experiences. Still another point in Vive's favor was that it was developed by the gaming marketplace Steam's parent company, Valve, portending a rich supply of compatible games and experiences for the Vive platform.

The prospect of bringing VR into our library raised questions about the technology's suitability for a makerspace. Though we were, and remain, actively conscious of VR applications suited to the production of creative works, the frank answer to such questions is that we craved more visitors. It was early days for this technology, and our students' access to room-scale VR was almost nil. Though the cost of the Dell PC and the Vive hardware far exceeded the makerspace's entire annual supply budget, our IT-savvy library director flinched not a bit at the exceptional request.

INSTALLATION AND INTEGRATION

The happy accident of a burgeoning makerspace with few machines and ample floor space made STEAMworks the perfect spot for KU's first foray into virtual reality.

We decided to site the Vive's play area—the usable space defined by its lighthouses—very near the room's entrance during most of the initial year. Passersby and users of an adjacent computer lab could plainly see and hear players experiencing VR. The Vive's proximity to the room's entrance encouraged impromptu drop-ins by people who, hearing laughter through our always-open door, decided to visit on a whim.

Reconfiguration is a constant in our young makerspace. By the end of the Vive's first year, we had moved the play area toward the back of the room to make way for a student-staffed reception desk near the door. In the process we took measures to reduce tripping hazards. Though first-generation Vive equipment employs multiple wireless technologies, its headset must connect to the CPU through a pair of physical cables that are ordinarily some fifteen feet long. In practice, this meant that portions of our room were arbitrarily fenced off according to a player's position, and that VR users in wheelchairs needed a spotter to actively clear the cables.

To enable our cabling to drop cleanly down from above to the Vive goggles requires running it through wall and ceiling cavities, doubling the length of its run. This is not a trivial exercise: latency can result from ill-chosen cables, and HTC offers no sanctioned extension kits.[5] Online discussants warned of unacceptable results for some consumer-grade cables whose lengths exceeded their signal-carrying capacity, but we found little consensus about fail-safe good ones at our price point. We were fortunate indeed when the second and third long cables we purchased worked without lag.

Most of our substantial library of games and experiences came to us free or at low cost. We have paid no more than thirty dollars for a few of them; in two instances, a student purchased game licenses on his own and gave them to the library.

WHAT THE IMPACT IS

VR has drawn other visitors besides college students to our room in the library; the Vive is a popular attraction for children visiting campus, and faculty kids as well; and though their parents have been slower to embrace this technology, exceptions are notable.

Browsing the SteamVR store occasionally turns up applications with rich instructional potential. When we find one, we reach out to our faculty in the relevant subject areas. For example, an experience titled *Eye of the Owl*, which is free of charge in the SteamVR store, brings users into the creepy virtual studio of the sixteenth-century painter Hieronymus Bosch, whose surreal triptych *The Garden of Earthly Delights* is a staple of KU's Art History survey course. We invited veteran art professors to give it a try. The one who did was enchanted: "I actually saw this painting in person, have taught it for years, but I'm seeing things now that I had never noticed!"

Similarly drawn by an interest in bringing VR to their students' learning experiences, faculty from disciplines including medieval history, physical anthropology, crafts, geology, commercial art, and biology have brought questions and expressed tentative interest. A few have been enticed to strap on the goggles themselves.

Several Steam titles that were in fact free, or nearly so, for us (*The VR Museum of Fine Art* and *The Night Café* are others), pull users into dazzling encounters with well-known artworks in ways that are perhaps better than real life. Our art history professor noted that she was forced to keep her distance when visiting Bosch's painting at the Prado Museum in Madrid, whereas VR facilitates convincingly realistic close-up inspection. As we hoped, she raved publicly about *Eye of the Owl* to the large audiences of students in her courses in art history. Many came to try the Vive and some *did* follow their teacher's suggestion to experience the Bosch "game," but even those students soon shifted to playing actual games.

Table 5.1 shows the most-used titles in our collection ranked by cumulative engagement time. (It should come as no surprise that Steam collects granular data about customers' habits; our VR computer runs on a generic account, apart from KU's IT access control system, hence these data cannot be disaggregated to the level of individual users.)

TABLE 5.1

Cumulative play time of top 25 VR games/experiences
at Kutztown University's STEAMworks, AY 2016–17

RANK, TITLE, STEAM APP ID NUMBER	PLAY TIME	RANK, TITLE, STEAM APP ID NUMBER	PLAY TIME
	Hours		*Hours*
1. Tilt Brush: 327140	78.2	14. Rick and Morty, Virtual Rick-ality: 469610	8.9
2. Job Simulator: 448280	72.7	15. Fantastic Contraption: 386690	7.1
3. Universe Sandbox: 230290	56.2	16. theBlu: 451520	6.8
4. The Lab: 450390	39.1	17. Surgeon Simulator VR, Meet The Medic: 457420	6.8
5. Google Earth VR: 348250	22.1	18. NVIDIA® VR Funhouse: 468700	6.5
6. Rec Room: 471710	18.3	19. Poly Runner VR: 462910	6.1
7. Accounting: 518580	18.3	20. Catlateral Damage: 329860	5.0
8. Waltz of the Wizard: 436820	15.3	21. The Body VR, Journey Inside a Cell: 451980	5.0
9. Eye of the Owl: 420020	12.0	22. Trials on Tatooine: 381940	4.9
10. The VR Museum of Fine Art: 515020	12.0	23. InCell VR: 396030	4.7
11. Keep Talking and Nobody Explodes: 341800	11.9	24. Wake Up: 499540	4.5
12. Spell Fighter VR: 455440	11.0	25. 3D Organon VR Anatomy: 548010	4.3
13. Break Time!: 578470	10.4		

NOTE: 525.92 total hours of play were logged on 78 different games, by 181 known users (147 KU students, 10 KU staff and faculty personnel, 9 unaffiliated adults, and 15 children under age 18)

Titles are likely to mislead the uninitiated. A career counselor would be stunned to hear *Job Simulator* coaching a neophyte auto mechanic to top up a car's "headlight fluid" in a cartoonish world run by robots; similarly, *The Lab* is about a lot of things, but the scientific method is not among them.

Perhaps the most consistently satisfying experience for us is that of seeing the immersive power of *Google Earth VR* to transport homesick people back to familiar neighborhoods with stunningly convincing realism. Watching an international student guide friends to Turkmenistan and fly over the roof of his house is astonishing, yet objectively no more so than seeing kids from nearby New Jersey pointing out their grade schools and playfields while gaining a new perspective on terrain they have known all their lives. Users have also pinned the location of Kutztown University's sprawling 300-acre campus,

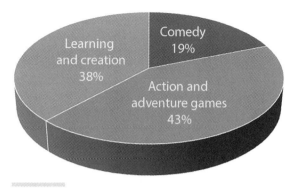

FIGURE 5.1
Engagement by type of VR experience

and in some cases they have expanded their consciousness of nonobvious features of our environs such as the nearby Hawk Mountain Sanctuary, Rodale Institute, and the Appalachian Trail. To an incoming Kutztown student, the nearby landscape might seem little more than tedious cornfields alternating with soybean fields. Many, perhaps most, never get beyond this shallow perception, but we have seen VR raise people's appreciation of their physical world.

The comparison in figure 5.1 of cumulative time spent with creative and educative titles, loosely defined, versus time inside games that are purely entertaining lays no claim to investigative rigor, but it is noteworthy that three games of the second category whose attraction is *humor* are wildly popular. Those three would have commanded an even higher share than 19 percent if not for our sententious delay, before finally caving shortly prior to the end of the school year, in acquiring the sensational *Virtual Rick-ality*.

Virtual reality users at Kutztown University's Rohrbach Library in AY 2016–17 spent slightly more than one-third of their time with experiences designed to teach or to furnish creative outlets, such as *The VR Museum of Fine Art, Google Blocks,* and *Tilt Brush.* Three other games coded here as "Comedy" all involve Owlchemy Labs of Austin (Texas) and/or Justin Roiland, cocreator of the animated series *Rick and Morty* on Cartoon Network's Adult Swim: *Job Simulator, Accounting,* and *Virtual Rick-ality.* (Their cumulative play time logged by all users was 3,155 minutes.)

Come for the Bosch and van Gogh, stay for the *Rick and Morty.* Clearly our Vive brings people to the library who would probably never have visited us otherwise. Still, the question lingers: *Converting a portion of a room in an academic library to a noisy game arcade—doesn't that demean the sanctity of higher education?*

Many older people who understand print on paper as the sine qua non for the transmission of knowledge about culture are hard-pressed to appreciate the true contours of a majestic, richly varied digital media landscape where

YouTube is a preferred learning tool, and where the works of vaguely familiar names like Kurosawa or Fellini might mean very little alongside those of Sid Meier and Shigeru Miyamoto, artists whose masterful creations are, by design, experienced differently by all even while profoundly imprinting shared histories in the minds of their audiences.

WHAT COMES NEXT

As of this writing in early 2018, popular enthusiasm for VR seems to have plateaued. It is fun but not life-changing; spectacular, but *Why is this stupid cord attached to my head?* Its next important hurdle—true wireless capability for affordable VR that leverages processing power beyond that of a smartphone—will soon be cleared. In addition, we can look forward to tremendously rich augmented reality (AR) and mixed reality hybrids.

AR technologies that weave digital artifacts into our physical surroundings feel like a step toward a customizable world. In a large building like our library, whose size is daunting to newcomers and denizens alike, it is easy to imagine how grand life will be with cheap, readily available AR headsets (or visors, or smart contact lenses) empowering users to unerringly navigate the place according to real-time needs and whims: when a student asks the headset where to find books about Tchaikovsky, the walls *she* sees will instantly fill with signs pointing her toward the ML410 shelves—signs that will melt away and be replaced when she asks about the nearest restroom, or the café.

A KU faculty member was among the first to obtain a developers' kit for Microsoft's HoloLens, a self-contained AR headset that evinces enormous potential. (See chapter 2.) The rig had seen very little use until STEAMworks student staff obtained permission to work up an entertaining demo for visiting high-schoolers: it filled a room with large 3D letters spelling HAPPY HALLOWEEN, plus goblins and jack-o'-lanterns. All went well, so the HoloLens found a home in our makerspace.

Some futurists risk muddling the conversation when they dismissively contrast today's VR with tomorrow's AR. Libraries ought not be discouraged from installing an affordable VR system for fear the technology is passé; instead, it is one of two exciting approaches that promise vastly different applications and capabilities. The *Eye of the Owl* VR experience of visiting Hieronymus Bosch's studio would be *less* interesting should the painter's workspace be superimposed on the tables and counters of your school's art room, AR-style, while familiar faces of bored classmates yawn and sneeze in front of the epic triptych. The total immersion that VR affords is entirely appropriate in this and many other instances.

One fascinating question that remains is an old one: what will developers—instructional designers among them, we should hope—*do* with VR and AR? The compelling realism of immersive technologies cries out for the work of artists with a stake in advancing pedagogy. There have already been highly promising attempts to leverage archaeological expertise in the VR space using photogrammetry, a set of techniques that stitches together snapshots to map precisely rendered digital scenes. The real trick, however, will be in monetizing such work. If institutions can somehow fund the development of deeply researched and truly engaging experiences that capture the interest of young scholars, an important corner will be turned.

But the production of high-quality VR experiences is time- and resource-intensive. Simply wrapping batches of content in technology associated with video gaming imparts to instructional software none of the visceral appeal of a well-designed first-person shooter, not even in VR. Powerful as the VR and AR media are, substantial challenges face those who would use them to enhance learning. Tremendous development environments such as Unity and Unreal Engine are easy to get, yet the skills and person-hours needed to produce truly riveting VR experiences are hard to come by. Although colleges and universities have talent to spare, they are vulnerable to real-world pressures. Market forces determine what must be taught and, ultimately, the types of jobs that skilled graduates must take in order to pay off their loans. Still, there will remain a niche for developers driven by idealism (and perhaps cushioned by wealth) to create compelling VR and AR learning objects while doubtless operating at a loss.

A key lesson our library has learned throughout this experiment is that spaces for the consumption and creation of new media are a welcome feature of library services, and are valued by users of various orientations. Those who have come to us because of VR represent a broad cross-section of the sorts of visitors we always hope to serve: studious nerds, athletic jocks, 'bros, trans kids, politics geeks, artists, conspiracy theorists, and normals. Plus everyone in between.

While VR in its current forms will seem laughably primitive in comparison to the increasingly sophisticated, ubiquitous AR hybrids of the 2020s and 2030s,[6] there is no evidence that today's enhanced platforms for the experiential consumption of realistic content—interactive storytelling—are some passing fad.

The library is a growing organism. Ranganathan's fifth law, a metaphor that still astonishes readers with its expressive power, is a comparative foray into vivid surrealism. One is hard-pressed to imagine the Indian scholar *not* embracing well-crafted software such as *Organon VR* as an awesome way to understand the human organism, and VR itself as yet another window through which library users can gaze with fresh eyes into their own humanity.

NOTES

1. Michael Ferguson, "Creating Common Ground: Shared Reading and the First Year of College" *Peer Review* 8, no. 3 (summer 2006): 8–10.

2. For Steam, the major online game marketplace, with tens of thousands of titles for a variety of devices and platforms. Its services are integrated with Vive and Oculus through SteamVR. Librarians could think of Steam as a flashier GOBI, but without the books.

3. Oliver Kreylos, "Lighthouse Tracking Examined," *Doc-OK.org* (blog), May 25, 2016, http://doc-ok.org/?p=1478.

4. The one complaint we *have* heard, an entirely predictable one, comes from certain Oculus owners who proudly proclaim the superiority of their awesome system.

5. A fully wireless Vive was well received at the 2017 Consumer Electronics Show in Las Vegas; HTC's website through much of the first half of that year touted its imminent release, but references to the system eventually disappeared. In fall 2018 the company finally released the Vive Wireless Adapter to consumers, priced at $300; we await delivery as this book goes to press. Untethered systems using less cumbersome belt-mounted hardware that connects to goggles via short cords or Bluetooth—an analog in the AR space is Magic Leap's tiny self-contained processor that obviates any need for a gaming computer— promise to remove what has been an awkward obstacle to seamlessly experiencing alternate realities.

6. When enthusiasts will create nostalgic retro-Vive and Throwbaculus experiences using coin-sized single-board computers with mirrored swim goggles from the dollar store.

MATT COOK and
ZACK LISCHER-KATZ

6

Integrating 3D and Virtual Reality into Research and Pedagogy in Higher Education

FOLLOWING A PERIOD OF EXPERIMENTATION STARTING IN THE LATE 1980s and continuing into the early 2000s, virtual reality technologies have returned to mainstream consciousness. The low cost and relative ease of use of today's technologies have effectively democratized VR, moving current research away from million-dollar CAVE systems—which are typically accessible only to computer science and engineering experts—to inexpensive, portable, head-mounted displays (HMDs) that anyone can use.[1] With the public release of the Oculus Rift headset in March 2016, followed closely by the HTC Vive in April 2016, high-fidelity VR has become affordable for a growing segment of the population. While this resurgence in VR was primarily sparked by the video-gaming market, educational institutions are enthusiastically exploring the benefits of newly obtainable VR technologies and are beginning to integrate them into academic research and instruction.[2]

At the same time that VR has become more accessible, the tools for creating high-resolution 3D models of cultural heritage sites and artifacts, biological specimens, medical imaging, and more are becoming more widely available. Indeed, photogrammetric processing software is poised to make every smartphone a potential 3D content creation tool and a mechanism for capturing and digitizing the physical world. This relationship—between a robust digital content type and an increasingly accessible display platform—has implications for classroom instruction and faculty research activities, especially where fragile, distant, or otherwise inaccessible objects are concerned.

By developing customized, discipline-agnostic VR tools for interacting with 3D content, the University of Oklahoma (OU) Libraries is leading the way in bringing VR and 3D technologies together in an academic library context. This chapter describes the experience of emerging technology librarians at OU Libraries, who have developed and deployed a public-facing VR platform for academic use, with the hope that the lessons learned will offer guidance to other library professionals considering VR for their institutions. The chapter begins with some background on the benefits of VR and an overview of the history of VR at OU Libraries, followed by a case study of an undergraduate-level VR course integration, and an assessment of the preservation and curation hurdles that hosting VR content brings to the library. The chapter concludes with a discussion of some of the future trends to watch as VR begins to shape the library of the future.

VIRTUAL REALITY AT THE UNIVERSITY OF OKLAHOMA

Virtual Reality in Libraries

The realistic nature of immersive virtual reality learning environments supports scholarship in new ways that are impossible with traditional two-dimensional displays (e.g., textbook illustrations, computer screens, etc.). Research in engineering, architecture, archaeology, and anatomy, among other fields, has demonstrated the benefits of VR for research and instruction.[3] The extent to which a virtual experience resembles its real-world counterpart—termed "fidelity" in the literature—has been studied under controlled conditions and demonstrates the broad applicability of the technology.[4] Researchers have identified a set of unique characteristics associated with high-fidelity VR systems that result in increased performance on tasks that require searching for, identifying, and describing the features of 3D content. These studies suggest that the increased field of regard and the perceived depth of the virtual environment, coupled with embodied interface mechanisms like head and hand tracking, allows users to perceive and act on visual cues that are typically lacking from a traditional computer workstation.

Virtual reality succeeds (or fails), then, insofar as it places the user in a learning environment within which the object of study can be analyzed as if that object were physically present and fully interactive in the user's near visual field.[5] These platform characteristics are most relevant to spatially oriented types of content, which makes researchers conclude that, for now, VR "lead[s] to better discovery in domains whose primary dimensions are spatial."[6] As the capabilities of VR expand beyond visual and spatial engagement, disciplines where compelling content might require realistic tactile, olfactory, or auditory sensation (e.g., in various humanities fields) will likewise be supported.

A Brief History of Virtual Reality at the University of Oklahoma

In fall 2014, a small group of faculty and library staff from the University of Oklahoma attended an Immersive Visualization "boot camp" workshop hosted by the Emerging Analytics Center at the University of Arkansas, Little Rock.[7] While there, attendees were introduced to a range of cutting-edge virtual reality tools, including a full-sized CAVE system and the newly released Oculus Developer Kit II (DK2), one of the earliest publicly available virtual reality HMDs. Upon returning to the Norman Campus, library staff rushed to order their own DK2. The library administration supported these early efforts, financially and with staff time, and saw the emergence of these new tools and associated innovation spaces as critical to maintaining the OU Libraries' position as the technological and intellectual crossroads of the university.

Fortunately, as a consumer device—generally geared towards the early-stage development of virtual reality gaming applications—the HMD hardware proved to be quite affordable (approximately $350) for an academic library, which meant that several units could be purchased and demonstrated in the main OU library. The following academic year, 2015, was defined by further experimentation and demonstration of the still-novel VR hardware, including "road show"–type setups as well as integration into larger library exhibits (e.g., the *Galileo's World* exhibit) and various on-campus technology fairs.[8] The response from students, faculty, staff, and the general public was almost universally positive.

By 2016, virtual reality had found a permanent home within OU Libraries, in the Innovation @ the EDGE Makerspace.[9] Existing relationships with several key OU faculty led to VR-assisted integrations in courses focused on spatially oriented content that was particularly conducive to analysis in virtual space. Biology, architecture, and fine art courses used the beta hardware within the Innovation @ the EDGE during the 2016 academic year.[10] Since then, fifteen distinct academic departments across campus have begun adopting library-supported VR course integrations.

The Oklahoma Virtual Academic Laboratory

During the first year of experimental adoption, the surge in positive feedback from faculty resulted in an unforeseen challenge for OU's emerging technology librarians: how does a small library unit develop educational software, on a case-by-case basis, for all interested researchers and instructors? Moreover, informal usability data—compiled using a customized version of John Brooks's System Usability Scale—revealed a host of user experience issues related primarily to hardware ergonomics.[11] The current high-end HMDs (e.g., Rift and Vive) still rely on tethered connection to a PC, and this cabling often interferes with the user's experience of immersion in the virtual space.[12] The use of hand tracking or other embodied controllers also had the tendency to bring the user into contact with physical obstructions, like a desk, keyboard, or nearby persons.[13]

In order to strategically manage the rising local demand, while accounting for practical problems like cable management and user range-of-motion, OU Libraries partnered with the University of Oklahoma's Physics Department, specifically their physics fabrication facility. There, a chair-on-rails assembly (see figure 6.1) was designed and implemented that complemented a custom

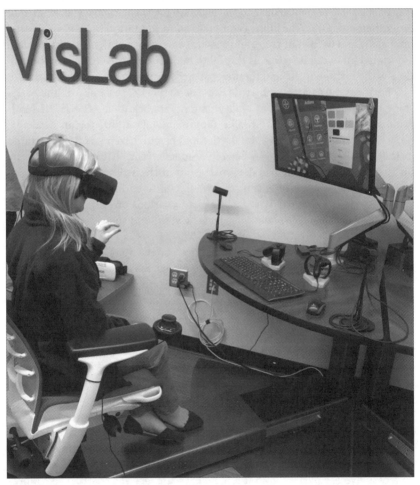

FIGURE 6.1
OVAL VR workstation in use

software package that would allow users to remotely upload 3D content to virtual reality for shared manipulation of that content across a network of Oculus Rift headsets. Thus was born the Oklahoma Virtual Academic Laboratory, or OVAL.

Course Integrations

By year three of OU Libraries' virtual reality initiative, eight networked OVAL workstations had been deployed across three locations on the Norman Campus, effectively forming a distributed virtual classroom in which faculty and students in different campus locations could teach and collaborate. Using OVAL, users were empowered to manipulate their 3D content, modify environmental conditions (such as lighting), annotate 3D models, and take accurate measurements, side-by-side with other students or their instructors (see figure 6.2). Moreover, specific departments began to engage with these systems at a deeper level, resulting in a core group of committed faculty who have seen virtual reality–supported course integrations continuing over multiple academic years. Students in architecture, anthropology, biochemistry, journalism, engineering, art and art history, library and information science, English, and law regularly engage with OVAL workstations as part of their coursework at the University of Oklahoma.

OU Libraries' collaboration with the university's Anthropology Department represents a paradigmatic use case insofar as the structure of this particular course integration was shown to be pedagogically effective and is transferable to other classes. In fall 2017, students in an introductory undergraduate anthropology class were given the opportunity to visit campus VR facilities and engage with hominid skull models (which were freely obtained through existing online 3D asset repositories, such as Morphosource and

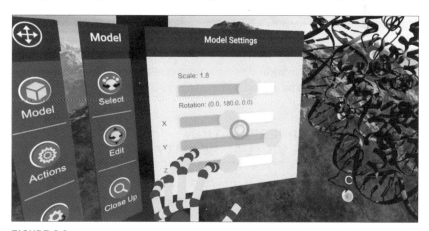

FIGURE 6.2
OVAL user interface, Version 1.0

African Fossils).[14] In preparation, emerging technology librarians worked with the course instructor to develop a course assignment that would leverage the documented benefits of the VR platform in support of the learning objectives of a particular course module. (See appendix for the activity that was used in the anthropology class.)

The questions in the assignment required the students to search for specific features on a virtual *Homo heidelbergensis* cranium, describe the structural changes evident in chronologically ordered fossils, and analyze specific skull features in order to determine diet.[15] The content being analyzed was both physically inaccessible to undergraduate students and spatially oriented, making for a particularly well-suited application of the VR technology. In effect, OU Libraries expanded access for undergraduates to fragile, distant specimens that they would otherwise have been unable to "handle" and learn from.

To evaluate the benefits of VR for student learning, the authors collected data in the form of pre- and post-surveys and semi-structured interviews with students following completion of the assignment. Initial analysis of the data collected suggests an improvement in students' self-efficacy in regard to their ability to carry out spatial analysis tasks.[16] This follows an earlier study in which VR was shown to positively impact scale perception, error recognition, creativity, and communication for architecture students.[17]

The VR-based anthropology assignment was specifically designed to support the learning objectives of the course module, and training time was provided for students to explore the OVAL software before the measured learning activity. Several practical takeaways can be drawn from this series of successful course integrations. For one thing, hygiene considerations have led us to upgrade all HMD facial interfaces to a disinfectable material, and student workers have been trained to regularly clean all HMD and workstation components. In addition, 3D model preparation tasks and discipline-specific workflows—related to the preprocessing of medical or chemical protein data sets, for example—have proven to be time-consuming.[18] Emerging technology librarians have learned from this and now work closely with faculty to establish realistic time lines in advance of a course integration, in order to allow for training, material preparation, and arranging breakout sessions (for when the class size is too large to be hosted in one of the visualization spaces all at once).

CURATION AND PRESERVATION CHALLENGES OF VIRTUAL REALITY

The sustainability of VR as a legitimate library resource depends on managing VR-related data and digital tools throughout the research life cycle or throughout the life cycle of teaching resources. Through working with 3D and VR in course integrations and in faculty research, OU Libraries staff have identified three critical curation areas in which the library should take the lead:

managing hardware and software obsolescence, archiving 3D file formats, and developing metadata standards.

Managing VR Hardware and Software Obsolescence

Technological obsolescence poses a serious threat to supporting VR as a sustainable academic tool. Because hardware and software configurations change over time, we risk losing access to current software if systems are not constantly updated, but this makes it increasingly difficult to access older software and content, which could have a significant impact on research reproducibility. For example, if researchers run an analysis using version 1.0 of a VR application, and then they run it on a later version, they could get different results.

To address some of these challenges, the emerging technologies library team has started to document changes made to the VR system over time, including any hardware and software updates and modifications. This documentation will help with configuring emulators in the future for making older VR software accessible.[19]

Moreover, when an instructor or researcher works with a VR system in an academic context, it is important that they know which version of the software and data is being used, who created it, and whether the 3D objects have been revised or otherwise changed. Research data platforms like Zenodo or Open Science Framework can be useful for archiving VR code and 3D models, and they issue persistent identifiers (DOIs, ARKs, etc.) which ensure that the research products produced through VR visualization are sustainable and citable.[20]

File Formats for Archiving 3D Content

One major issue that still remains unresolved in the 3D modeling world is the lack of standardized file formats for archiving 3D models. The ubiquitous OBJ files format has become a de facto standard, despite its limitations, and most software packages are able to import and export it without a problem. It is a simple format, typically encoded in ASCII, so it can be easily viewed in a text editor. The main downside of this format is that it does not have any capabilities for embedding metadata into its file, and texture and color information have to be stored in separate files. To address this, the emerging technologies team has been experimenting with the COLLADA file format (.dae file type). This is an XML-based format that has a capacity for embedding metadata in its header, which is particularly useful for embedding calibration information into the model file, enabling for accurate measurements of the model within the VR platform. There is also discussion in the library field about using X3D as a preservation format. X3D is an ISO standard maintained by the Web3D Consortium, and supersedes the VRML format, which was developed in the 1990s to make 3D content accessible on the Internet.[21]

Metadata for VR Content

The establishment of metadata standards is another area in which communities of 3D model creators and digital curators are still trying to find consensus. A few projects have tried to develop metadata guidelines, but these have not been widely adopted, nor do they easily translate into schemas for existing preservation repositories that libraries and archives might already have installed.[22] Because the creation of 3D models involves many technical steps and points at which the creator needs to make decisions, the precision and accuracy of a model cannot be entirely judged from the end result alone. Instead, researchers must have access to information about how the model was created.[23]

Current Projects Addressing Preservation and Curation Challenges

There are several projects in the field that are currently addressing these preservation and curation challenges, including the PARTHENOS (Pooling Activities, Resources and Tools for Heritage E-research Networking, Optimization and Synergies) Project, which is working with cultural institutions across Europe to develop standards and best practices for curating 3D content; and three National Leadership Grant projects that received funding in 2017 from the Institute for Museum and Library Services to bring together experts in the field in order to develop standards and best practices for 3D and VR.[24] These ongoing projects suggest that standards and best practices for 3D/VR will likely see growing stabilization and consensus over the next two to three years, making it important to monitor these developments when implementing a 3D and VR program.

FUTURE DIRECTIONS FOR VIRTUAL REALITY

VR and 3D technologies are beginning to support exciting new applications in an increasing range of educational contexts. VR HMDs and 3D scanning hardware and software continue to drop in price, suggesting that more and more institutions, such as K–12 education, public libraries, and museums, will find these technologies increasingly feasible to adopt. Improvements in technology are also promising, as graphics-processing hardware—currently, NVidia 10-series GPUs and their equivalents—are surpassing the 60+ frames-per-second threshold that is necessary to enable longer periods of VR use by the casual user without nausea or eyestrain. Finally, professional-grade 3D modeling and VR data visualization software are being adopted into more and more industries, which suggests that the integration of virtual reality into the day-to-day workflows of scholars may be imminent.[25] This combination of cost, hardware capabilities, and "killer apps" means that more disciplines and areas of research will begin adopting virtual reality as an accepted tool of the trade.

For a variety of disciplines, VR technology and 3D content can also provide the necessary infrastructure for multiuser events in which professors, teachers, and curators will be able to facilitate classes, tours, and exhibitions for geographically dispersed participants in virtual reality.[26] For example, an expert could lead a tour through a highly detailed 3D model of Stonehenge, move the virtual sun in the virtual sky, and discuss how the site was built in relation to solar events. This technology shows great promise for distance learning. There are innumerable other types of curated tours and exhibits that could be imagined and executed in a virtual space that would both provide access to otherwise inaccessible sites and artifacts and bring together participants from all over the world.

Other important trends to monitor include the development of web-based and mobile VR, the development of new repositories and search tools for accessing federated collections of 3D models, and the role of VR and AR (augmented reality) in shaping the library of the future.

Web-Based Virtual Reality

As VR software moves to the Web it will support the development of mobile-based VR, and make development easier and more sustainable. The release of WebVR in March 2016 enabled Chrome and Firefox web browsers to serve VR content to any current HMD. Using a web browser rather than hardware-specific software reduces some of the aforementioned obsolescence problems and promotes the interoperability of content across different manufacturers' HMDs. It is also important to monitor ongoing standardization initiatives, such as the work being conducted by the Khronos Group and its OpenXR project, which is working with the major HMD producers to develop common standards for connecting HMDs to computers.[27]

Repositories and Discovery

Another trend to follow is the development of repositories for 3D content and new tools for searching through and browsing 3D collections. Because of the growing demand for access and the high cost of producing accurate, high-resolution 3D models, institutions will need to develop shared repositories, federated search engines, and other tools for searching across collections. Existing academic collections of 3D models, including Morphosource, African Fossils, and NIH 3D Print Exchange, as well as commercial sites that host increasing amounts of academic content, such as Sketchfab, have begun to spring up online.[28] Institutions such as the University of Wyoming, the University of Virginia, and the Smithsonian Institution have begun to experiment with integrating 3D models into existing repository systems.[29] In addition, discussion has begun in the International Image Interoperability Framework (IIIF) community about the need to develop a similar set of APIs for displaying 3D models online.[30]

For easily embedding 3D content in a website, and making it accessible to VR equipment, the Sketchfab commercial platform is leading the way.[31] The open-source, web-based 3D presenter tool 3D-HOP (3D Heritage Online Presenter), developed by the Visual Computing Lab of ISTI-CNR, adds more analytic tools for the web-based display of 3D models, but it requires additional development and servers to deploy.[32] Large-scale collections of 3D content will become increasingly important as the means for students and researchers to access, archive, and analyze 3D models.

Once some desirable combination of 3D database characteristics has been developed and deployed to support scholarship, the browsing process can feed back into, and be further augmented by, virtual reality. Here we come quite close to Michael Buckland's conception of "information-as-thing," whereby evidential objects in the world constitute "primary sources."[33] In VR, browseable virtual collections of high-quality 3D objects can surround users as spatially oriented arrays of information artifacts, enabling the researcher to not only explore textual resources, but analyze precise digital copies of specimens, artifacts, and other forms of research data.[34]

Beyond the Near Future

How will VR fit into the library of the more distant future? Given current trends, we expect to see a number of developments over the next 5–10 years. AR and VR technologies will merge, the resulting hardware will become as ubiquitous as the smartphone, and the library will become responsible for the organization, preservation, and accessibility of 3D digital collections, just as it currently is responsible for printed and electronic texts and images. Rather than passively hosting 3D models and VR technologies in their libraries, trained library staff will actively support research and instruction by developing new applications and specialized features for VR across disciplines. The academic library will continue to promote interdisciplinarity and support research and instruction by simultaneously establishing new research and teaching methods and making the latest tools and advanced digital infrastructures accessible, enabling faculty to lead VR class sessions with students dispersed all over the world.

CONCLUSION

Our experiences deploying VR across the University of Oklahoma campus, with the library as the central facilitator, have demonstrated the value of these new tools. With the growth of 3D modeling and other 3D content creation tools, and the need for students to develop spatial cognitive skills in a variety of fields, VR becomes the ideal platform for students and researchers to analyze 3D materials in their full three dimensions.[35]

While VR still has a few years to go before it loses its "wow factor" and becomes an established academic tool, the day is not far off when online and face-to-face classes will be conducted, in part or in total, in VR, and researchers will be able to travel to archaeological digs halfway across the world or analyze scientific specimens from the comfort of their ubiquitous VR devices. VR is poised to expand the library's mission by enhancing access to information resources and providing new analytic tools that promote spatial understanding and embodied analysis in an academic world that is still too often ruled by the flatness of text and two-dimensional images.

APPENDIX

Fall 2017 Anthropology VR Assignment

Anthropology ANTH1113 Activity—VR Study

1. Looking at the specimen *Homo heidelbergensis,* several features are labeled; match these labels to the features. Note that there are more labels than features.

    _____ Foramen magnum

    _____ Zygomatic arch

    _____ Supraorbital torus

2. Prognathism refers to the length of the face (how much of a snout is retained). Examine the specimens labeled early, middle, and late and describe how prognathism changes over time.

3. Recall that dentition (dental arcade) is highly responsive to diet, and that softer diets will lead to more V-shaped and more compacted dental arcades.

    Look at the species labeled A and B and explain why you think one had a tougher diet than the other.

NOTES

1. CAVE refers to CAVE Automatic Virtual Environment, a room-sized virtual reality space that uses multiple video projectors and head-tracking sensors to produce an immersive and stereoscopic experience for the user. It was first proposed and developed by Carolina Cruz-Neira et al., "The CAVE: Audio Visual Experience Automatic Virtual Environment," *Communications of the ACM* 25, no. 6 (1992): 64–72.

2. Meredith Thompson, "Making Virtual Reality a Reality in Today's Classrooms," January 11, 2018, https://thejournal.com/Articles/2018/01/11/Making-Virtual-Reality-a-Reality-in-Todays-Classrooms.aspx?Page=4.

3. See Antonieta Angulo, "On the Design of Architectural Spatial Experiences Using Immersive Simulation," *Conference Proceedings, Envisioning Architecture: Design, Evaluation, Communication* (2013): 151–58; Abhishek Seth et al., "Virtual Reality for Assembly Methods Prototyping: A Review," *Virtual Reality* 15, no. 1 (2011): 5–20; Susan Jang et al., "Direct Manipulation Is Better Than Passive Viewing for Learning Anatomy in a Three-Dimensional Virtual Reality Environment," *Computers & Education* 106 (2017): 150–65; Andries van Dam, "Experiments in Immersive Virtual Reality for Scientific Visualization," *Computers & Graphics* 26, no. 4 (2002): 535–55.

4. Bireswar Laha et al., "Effects of VR System Fidelity on Analyzing Isosurface Visualization of Volume Datasets," *IEEE Transactions on Visualization and Computer Graphics* 20, no. 4 (2014): 513–22; Eric D. Ragan et al., "Studying the Effects of Stereo, Head Tracking, and Field of Regard on a Small-Scale Spatial Judgment Task," *IEEE Transactions on Visualization and Computer Graphics* 19, no. 5 (2013): 886–96.

5. Today's hardware will fail to resolve useful depth cues beyond certain virtual distances, according to Mike Alger, "Visual Design Methods for Virtual Reality," last modified September 2015, http://aperturesciencellc.com/vr/VisualDesignMethodsforVR_MikeAlger.pdf.

6. Ciro Donalek et al., "Immersive and Collaborative Data Visualization Using Virtual Reality Platforms," in *Proceedings of 2014 IEEE International Conference on Big Data* (2014): 609–14.

7. Bill Sherman, "Little Rock Immersive Visualization Bootcamp," last modified November 7, 2014, http://wiki.iq-station.com/index.php?title=Bootcamp_UALR.

8. "The University of Oklahoma Celebrates 125 Years with Statewide 'Galileo's World' Exhibition," press release, April 24, 2015, https://lib.ou.edu/documents/OU%20Galileo%27s%20World%20press%20release.pdf.

9. Meg Lloyd, "A Hub for Innovation and Learning," *Campus Technology* (January 1, 2018), https://campustechnology.com/articles/2018/01/31/a-hub-for-innovation-and-learning.aspx.

10. Matt Enis, "University of Oklahoma Expands Networked Virtual Reality Lab," *Library Journal* (August 2016), http://lj.libraryjournal.com/2016/08/

academic-libraries/university-of-oklahoma-expands-networked-virtual
-reality-lab/.

11. Aaron Bangor et al., "An Empirical Evaluation of the System Usability Scale," *International Journal of Human–Computer Interaction* 24, no. 6 (2008): 574–94.

12. Doug Bowman and Ryan McMahan, "Virtual Reality: How Much Immersion Is Enough?" *Computer* 40, no. 7 (2007), 36-43.

13. Lisa Castaneda et al., "Applied VR in the Schools, 2016–2017 Aggregated Report," Foundry 10, http://foundry10.0rg/wp-content/uploads/2017/09/All-School-Aggregated-Findings-2016–2017.pdf.

14. Doug Boyer, "Virtual Fossils Revolutionize the Study of Human Evolution," Aeon (2016), https://aeon.co/ideas/virtual-fossils-revolutionise-the-study
-of-human-evolution.

15. *Homo heidelbergensis,* Cranium, EA-DCC-03, Evolutionary Anthropology, Duke University, Durham, NC, www.morphosource.org/Detail/MediaDetail/Show/media_id/6233.

16. Zack Lischer-Katz and Matt Cook, "Evaluating Virtual Reality Use in Academic Library-Supported Course Integrations: Methodology and Initial Findings" (poster presentation at the Association for Library and Information Science Education Annual Conference, Denver, CO, February 2018), https://hdl.handle.net/11244/54431.

17. Elizabeth Pober and Matt Cook, "The Design and Development of an Immersive Learning System for Spatial Analysis and Visual Cognition," in *Proceedings of Conference of the Design Communication Association (2016)*, Bozeman, MT, September 7–10, 2016, www.designcommunication association.org/publications_proceedings.html.

18. Yifan Liu et al., "Workflows of Exporting Revit Models to Unity," report by Penn State CIC Research Group, last modified June 26, 2016, https://bim .wikispaces.com/file/view/Revit_3DS_Unity+Workflow.pdf.

19. Emulation involves using software to replicate an earlier operating system configuration in order to run older software that is no longer compatible with existing systems. For instance, an emulator could be used to run a piece of Mac OS6 software on a current Mac system.

20. Open Science Framework (https://osf.io/) and Zenodo (https://zenodo.org/) are both free platforms for documenting and archiving research data and related scholarly products.

21. For more information about the .x3d format, refer to www.web3d.org/x3d/what-x3d.

22. In their report "Digital 3D Objects in Art and Humanities: Challenges of Creation, Interoperability and Preservation," the PARTHENOS Project identified six metadata schemas that could be useful for documenting 3D models: Augmented Representation of Cultural Objects (ARCO), CARARE 2.0 (3D ICONS), CRMdig, LIDO, METS, and STARC Metadata Schema (https://hal.inria.fr/hal-01526713/file/White_Paper_3D_Parthenos_23052017

.pdf). Work has also been done by the 3D-COFORM Project (https://www
.brighton.ac.uk/research-and-enterprise/groups/computing/3d-coform.aspx)
and the Archaeological Data Service (http://guides.archaeologydataservice
.ac.uk/g2gp/CreateData_1–2) to develop metadata guidelines for 3D model
creation and description.

23. A set of principles for establishing transparency and trust for digitally
constructed 3D models of cultural heritage sites and artifacts was codified in
2006 in the London Charter, now in its second version: www.londoncharter
.org/introduction.html.

24. "PARTHENOS Project Report," www.parthenos-project.eu/digital-3d
-object-in-art-humanities/. The three IMLS-funded projects are "Developing
Library Strategy for 3D and Virtual Reality Collection Development and
Reuse," a partnership between Virginia Tech, Indiana University, and the
University of Oklahoma (https://lib.vt.edu/research-learning/lib3dvr.html);
"Community Standards for 3D Data Preservation," a partnership between
Washington University in St. Louis, the University of Michigan, and the
University of Iowa (http://gis.wustl.edu/dgs/community-standards-for
-3d-preservation-cs3dp-nation-forum-1-f1/); and "Building for Tomorrow:
Collaborative Development of Sustainable Infrastructure for Architectural
and Design Documentation," at the Frances Loeb Library at the Harvard
University Graduate School of Design (https://projects.iq.harvard.edu/
buildingtomorrow).

25. "Developer Spotlight: Using Oculus Medium in Production," https://www
.youtube.com/watch?v=KGgA6Q9EB4Y.

26. Dian Schaffhauser, "Multi-Campus VR Session Tours Remote Cave Art,"
Campus Technology (October 9, 2017), https://campustechnology.com/
articles/2017/10/09/multi-campus-vr-session-tours-remote-cave-art.aspx.

27. More information about the OpenXR project can be found at https://www
.khronos.org/openxr/.

28. For more information on these sites, see Morphosource (www.morpho
source.org/); African Fossils (http://africanfossils.org/); NIH 3D Print
Exchange (https://3dprint.nih.gov/); and Sketchfab (https://sketchfab
.com/).

29. For more information on the project at the University of Wyoming that
is integrating 3D content into its Islandora-based repository, see this
presentation by Chad Hutchens, head of digital collections: https://vimeo
.com/218636796. The University of Virginia has been making its 3D content
available via a 3DHOP deployment (e.g., http://fralin3d.iath.virginia.edu/
node/25) and through its data catalog (e.g., https://dataverse.lib.virginia
.edu/dataset.xhtml?persistentId=doi%3A10.18130/V3/3I825Q). For more
information about work being conducted at the Smithsonian Institution
to develop a repository for 3D models, see http://dpo.si.edu/blog/
scaling-3d-digitization-smithsonian.

30. The IIIF (http://iiif.io/) establishes a set of APIs (application programming interfaces) for describing and providing access to still images via the Web. It makes provisions for scaling and structural metadata, among other tools. Establishing a set of standardized protocols for accessing images online makes it possible for any IIIF-compliant viewer or application to accurately display any online collections that have been made accessible with the IIIF APIs.

31. 3D scanning projects produce very high-resolution models, which need to be "decimated," a form of data reduction, to be viewable in VR or online. Libraries need to make low-resolution 3D models easily accessible via online platforms, while maintaining the high-resolution models for scholarly analysis.

32. According to its website (http://vcg.isti.cnr.it/3dhop/), "3DHOP is an open-source software package for the creation of interactive Web presentations of high-resolution 3D models, oriented to the Cultural Heritage field."

33. Michael Buckland, "Information as Thing," *Journal of the American Society for Information Science* 42, no. 5 (1991): 351.

34. For a discussion of embodied browsing in virtual stacks, see Matt Cook, "Virtual Serendipity: Preserving Embodied Browsing Activity in the 21st Century Research Library," *Journal of Academic Librarianship* 44, no. 1 (2018): 145–49, https://doi.org/10.1016/j.acalib.2017.09.003.

35. VR could also contribute to developing students' spatial cognitive skills in other fields, such as engineering and mathematics, as defined in Sheryl Sorby, "Developing Spatial Cognitive Skills among Middle School Students," *Cognitive Processing* 10 (2009): S312–15; and Sheryl Sorby et al., "The Role of Spatial Training in Improving Spatial and Calculus Performance in Engineering Students," *Learning and Individual Differences* 26 (2013): 20–29.

BIBLIOGRAPHY

Alger, Mike. "Visual Design Methods for Virtual Reality." Last modified September 2015. http://aperturesciencellc.com/vr/VisualDesignMethodsforVR_MikeAlger.pdf.

Angulo, Antonieta. "On the Design of Architectural Spatial Experiences Using Immersive Simulation." In *Proceedings of the EAEA 11 Conference, Envisioning Architecture: Design, Evaluation, Communication*, 151–58. Milan, Italy, September 25–28, 2013. Rome: Edizioni Nuova Cultura 2013.

Bangor, Aaron, Philip T. Kortum, and James T. Miller. "An Empirical Evaluation of the System Usability Scale." *International Journal of Human–Computer Interaction* 24, no. 6 (2008): 574–94.

Bowman, Doug A., and Ryan P. McMahan. "Virtual Reality: How Much Immersion Is Enough?" *Computer* 40, no. 7 (2007): 36-43.

Boyer, D. "Virtual Fossils Revolutionize the Study of Human Evolution." Aeon. Last modified February 25, 2016. https://aeon.co/ideas/virtual-fossils-revolutionise-the-study-of-humanevolution.

Buckland, Michael K. "Information as Thing." *Journal of the American Society for Information Science* 42, no. 5 (1991): 351–60.

Castaneda, Lisa, A. Cechony, and A. Bautista. "Applied VR in the Schools, 2016–2017: Aggregated Report." Report by Foundry 10. September 2017. http://foundry10.0rg/wp-content/uploads/2017/09/All-School-Aggregated-Findings-2016–2017.pdf.

Cook, Matt. "Virtual Serendipity: Preserving Embodied Browsing Activity in the 21st Century Research Library." *Journal of Academic Librarianship* 44, no. 1 (2018): 145–49. https://doi.org/10.1016/j.acalib.2017.09.003.

Cruz-Neira, Carolina, Daniel J. Sandin, Thomas A. DeFanti, Robert V. Kenyon, and John C. Hart. "The CAVE: Audio Visual Experience Automatic Virtual Environment." *Communications of the ACM* 35, no. 6 (1992): 64–73.

Donalek, Ciro, George Djorgovski, A. Cioc, A. Wang, J. Zhang, E. Lawler, S. Yeh, et al. "Immersive and Collaborative Data Visualization Using Virtual Reality Platforms." In *Proceedings of 2014 IEEE International Conference on Big Data* (2014): 609–14.

Enis, Matt. "University of Oklahoma Expands Networked Virtual Reality Lab." *Library Journal,* August 2016. http://lj.libraryjournal.com/2016/08/academic-libraries/university-of-oklahoma-expands-networked-virtual-reality-lab/.

Jang, Susan, Jonathan M. Vitale, Robert W. Jyung, and John B. Black. "Direct Manipulation Is Better Than Passive Viewing for Learning Anatomy in a Three-Dimensional Virtual Reality Environment." *Computers & Education* 106 (2017): 150–65.

Laha, Bireswar, Doug A. Bowman, and John J. Socha. "Effects of VR System Fidelity on Analyzing Isosurface Visualization of Volume Datasets." *IEEE Transactions on Visualization and Computer Graphics* 20, no. 4 (2014): 513–22.

Lischer-Katz, Zack, and Matt Cook. "Evaluating Virtual Reality Use in Academic Library-Supported Course Integrations: Methodology and Initial Findings." Poster presentation at the Association for Library and Information Science Education Annual Conference, Denver, CO, February 2018. https://hdl.handle.net/11244/54431.

Liu, Yifan, et al. "Workflows of Exporting Revit Models to Unity." Report by Penn State CIC Research Group. Last modified June 26, 2016. https://bim.wikispaces.com/file/view/Revit_3DS_Unity+Workflow.pdf.

Lloyd, Meg. "A Hub for Innovation and Learning." *Campus Technology,* January 31, 2018. https://campustechnology.com/articles/2018/01/31/a-hub-for-innovation-and-learning.aspx.

Pober, Elizabeth, and Matt Cook. "The Design and Development of an Immersive Learning System for Spatial Analysis and Visual Cognition." In *Proceedings of Conference of the Design Communication Association,* Bozeman, MT, September 7–10, 2016. www.designcommunicationassociation.org/publications_proceedings.html.

Ragan, Eric D., Regis Kopper, Philip Schuchardt, and Doug A. Bowman. "Studying the Effects of Stereo, Head Tracking, and Field of Regard on a Small-Scale Spatial Judgment Task." *IEEE Transactions on Visualization and Computer Graphics* 19, no. 5 (2013): 886–96.

Schaffhauser, Dian. "Multi-Campus VR Session Tours Remote Cave Art." *Campus Technology,* October 9, 2017. https://campustechnology.com/articles/2017/10/09/multi-campus-vr-session-tours-remote-cave-art.aspx.

Seth, Abhishek, Judy M. Vance, and James H. Oliver. "Virtual Reality for Assembly Methods Prototyping: A Review." *Virtual Reality* 15, no. 1 (2011): 5–20.

Sherman, Bill. "Little Rock Immersive Visualization Bootcamp." Last modified November 7, 2014. http://wiki.iq-station.com/index.php?title=Bootcamp_UALR.

Sorby, Sheryl. "Developing Spatial Cognitive Skills among Middle School Students," *Cognitive Processing* 10 (2009): S312–15.

Sorby, Sheryl, Beth Casey, Norma Veurink, and Alana Dulaney. "The Role of Spatial Training in Improving Spatial and Calculus Performance in Engineering Students." *Learning and Individual Differences* 26 (2013): 20–29.

Thompson, Meredith. "Making Virtual Reality a Reality in Today's Classrooms." *THE Journal,* January 11, 2018. https://thejournal.com/articles/2018/01/11/making-virtual-reality-a-reality-in-todays-classrooms.aspx.

Van Dam, Andries, David H. Laidlaw, and Rosemary Michelle Simpson. "Experiments in Immersive Virtual Reality for Scientific Visualization." *Computers & Graphics* 26, no. 4 (2002): 535–55.

FELICIA A. SMITH

7

Information Literacy Instruction Using Virtual Reality

THIS CHAPTER EXPLORES THE POSSIBILITY OF ADDING VIRTUAL reality to library instruction as a way to make it more engaging. Virtual reality is a computer-generated technology that uses headgear to create a simulated world that enables users to interact with visual and auditory elements rendered or projected through the headgear. Traditional lecture-based approaches are no longer adequate for classroom instruction, so using active learning techniques is one method for improving learning and retention. A 2009 article explains why professors are moving away from lecture formats at respected institutions such as MIT, the Rensselaer Polytechnic Institute, North Carolina State University, the University of Maryland, the University of Colorado at Boulder, and Harvard.[1]

Physics professors at these institutions have been pioneering teaching methods rooted in research showing that most students learn fundamental concepts more successfully and apply them better through interactive, collaborative, student-centered learning. This article reported that the failure rate for lecture courses was between 10–12 percent. Not surprisingly, the failure rate dropped to only 4 percent after the physics professors switched to active learning methods.

One of the physics professors mentioned in the above article is Stanford University's Nobel laureate Carl Wieman. On May 25, 2017, Wieman was interviewed by KQED's Forum. Wieman explained his longtime mission to transform undergraduate education by ending one of its longest-standing traditions—the lecture. He has been studying effective teaching strategies for years. After his lectures, he found that only 10 percent of students retained the lecture material, based on their quiz results. Wieman's research found that active learning, in which students solve a specific problem, works better.[2]

While Wieman is focused on the long-standing issue of ineffective lectures, Stanford's education professor Sam Wineburg is studying a newer problem, that of "fake news." In this age of fake news, it can be hard to distinguish credible sources from clickbait websites. I met with Wineburg after he gained worldwide acclaim for conducting what the November 2016 issue of the *Wall Street Journal* called "the biggest [study] so far on how teens evaluate information they find online." Of the 7,804 students from middle school through college, Wineburg discovered that as many as 90 percent had trouble judging the credibility of the news.[3] Wineburg and I are both concerned that fake news is an ominous threat looming in the expansive digital information universe, and students are not properly trained to identify and assess this peril.

Stanford University's administration expects innovation from its employees. The Stanford Libraries are known for adopting emerging technologies that redefine students' educational experience. After Carl Wieman and I discussed our shared concern that traditional instruction methods are no longer adequate, I embarked upon a proposal to use emerging technology to address that concern in library classes. My proposal uses virtual reality to allow students to solve specific problems, as suggested by Wieman. I am proposing using VR to teach information literacy skills to undergraduates. This is an active learning alternative to lectures, with the added bonus of combating fake news. After discussions with both of the aforementioned Stanford professors, this was a logical proposal. The main objective of my VR project is to illustrate that the "common sense" used in everyday real life is the same as the "critical evaluation skillset" that is needed in the academic world.

One-way communication is not the future of instruction, but instead is an uninspired remnant of the past. Unfortunately, professors in academia teach in the same manner that they were taught. This lamentable dynamic results in overreliance on the traditional classroom lecture. Sadly, the traditional instructional approach is at best inadequate, and at worst an obstacle to deep and meaningful discovery. Regrettably, the outdated lecture has remained unchanged in libraries, as it has in the larger academic setting. Currently, library instruction workshops rely too heavily on the lecture format. There is a need for library instruction to evolve in order to maintain its relevance.

LITERATURE REVIEW

There are hundreds of findings to support the need for new and interactive teaching strategies. Lectures are not simply relics of the past; they are also boring and less effective than active learning approaches. It is safe to assume that most people have suffered through a lecturer droning on and on, seemingly endlessly. To test the hypothesis that lecturing maximizes learning and classroom performance, a group of researchers conducted a meta-analysis of 225 studies that reported data on examination scores or failure rates when comparing student performance in undergraduate science, technology, engineering, and mathematics (STEM) courses using traditional lecturing versus active learning. Their results revealed that students in classes with traditional lecturing were 1.5 times more likely to fail than were students in classes with active learning.

The STEM meta-analysis and the physics professors' findings can be extrapolated to library instruction, in which the traditional classroom lecture format has become similarly antiquated. Much as we no longer use horse-drawn buggies or steam locomotives to cross large distances, or send telegraph messages across the ocean, we should no longer rely on nineteenth-century methods for classroom instruction. The results are the same—we travel and communicate across great distances—even though we have greatly improved the effectiveness and performance of the tools we use. The mobile phones of today serve the same function as the landline phones in the twentieth century, but mobile phones have been enhanced with vastly superior capabilities as a result of the addition of powerful computing technologies. Likewise, technological advances should mean similar advances in the classroom.

One example of the superior capabilities of virtual reality is that it gives students the ability to interact with three-dimensional (3D) virtual representation and visualize abstract concepts, as opposed to just hearing unfamiliar, jargon-laden terminology. Students are then able to demonstrate their understanding of the lesson material by manipulating objects in the virtual environment. The students can benefit from immediate feedback, without the added pressure of classmates or instructors monitoring their progress. Instructors can also take advantage of data gathered at the completion of student sessions if they have designed features to capture the amount of incorrect selections.

Virtual reality is one way to incorporate powerful computing technology into information literacy instruction. This type of drastic enhancement for instruction is similar to the enhancements of telephones. Both are greatly improved as a result of the addition of computing technology. VR is the same type of teaching but is a newer model and is more engaging than lectures. Underneath the new shiny bells and whistles, my proposal is steeped in pedagogical gaming theories. Virtual reality utilizes an experiential learning approach wherein students use personal experiences (as opposed to books and lectures) to conceptualize and apply the knowledge being conveyed. This approach gives ownership to students and offers them the opportunity to manage their own learning. Virtual reality is an example of constructivist learning because it provides a highly interactive environment for active learning and is student-centric and focuses on meeting students' needs.

There is not a lot of research involving the use of virtual reality in academic library orientation, and particularly in one-shot type instructional workshops. The literature deals mostly with medical or flight types of simulations, which require practiced precision. There are some relevant articles that relate to generalized learning and virtual reality. For instance, Santos and Esposo-Betan published an article in 2018 highlighting the difficulty in showing the impact of mixed, virtual, or augmented reality. They explain that one reason why evidence-gathering is so problematic is due in large part to the lack of research material regarding such technologies because they are new and still developing.

Another article reports on the effects of interactive computer-based games and simulations and found statistically significant positive impacts on learning outcomes.[4] This meta-analysis goes on to explain that there is very little systemically analyzed evidence, in the literature, that discusses the effectiveness of virtual reality-based instruction in the context of the retention and transfer of learning from the virtual to the real environment.

OPPORTUNITIES

At one point, in the not so distant past, electronic books and articles were considered fanciful by people who are strict traditionalists. However, now it is nearly impossible to envisage teaching without digital media resources. In this same manner, virtual reality is about to revolutionize teaching. It is conceivable that we will tell future generations stories about how "back in my day, students were limited to being essentially locked inside of physical, mustard-colored, windowless classrooms, and were forced to listen to people talking to them for hours at a time, as the only means of instruction."

I posit that yet another problem with lecture-based instruction is the use of unfamiliar jargon that prevents comprehension of concepts. In addition to introducing new concepts, lectures involve jargon that further complicates the lesson. Students are being introduced to unfamiliar words describing abstract ideas that are not tied to any personal experience to which students can relate the concepts of the lesson. In contrast, using virtual reality, students will immediately translate real-life experiences into a comparable academic experience so that the academic lesson/concept can be associated with a realistic, personalized, and memorable experience. VR allows for a wondrous setting, without limitations, that can make a visually stunning first impression, which is vital for keeping learners engaged.

VR can be advantageous as a way to utilize a flipped-classroom curriculum, whereby the VR headgear and information literacy program is housed in a designated library area, outside of the classroom space. Students would be able to access the program when it is convenient for them. Ideally, the students would use the program at a time when they are receptive to learning, as opposed to during a mandated, scheduled library workshop. I have seen a lot of sleepy students struggling to stay awake during library workshops. Flipping the classroom would allow those students to embark upon the learning program when they are fully awake, which for me personally is late into the evening. I am not a morning person, so I do not learn in the best manner, during early morning sessions, when a lot of library workshops are scheduled.

Regardless of when or where students access the program, their learning objectives for this project are similar to those for traditional information literacy lessons, even with the addition of virtual reality technology. Upon completion, participants will be able to:

- Identify the information needed.
- Formulate appropriate question(s) based on the identified information need.
- Use credible information sources (in this case, common sense) to evaluate the need and get the desired outcome.

In addition to being able to flip the classroom, there are other advantages of virtual reality–based instruction. VR provides an amazing opportunity to develop new worlds and create personalized scenarios, an opportunity that is unparalleled in library instruction. VR is not just newer and shinier, but it is more engrossing than merely playing games purely for entertainment purposes. VR offers students the opportunity to erase physical boundaries and explore unknown worlds. Librarians can create real-life situations but present them in dazzling futuristic settings. The possibilities are endless.

VR allows instructors to create problems for students to solve that are familiar and relatable. It is a safe space for them to make incorrect choices without time limit pressures and without worrying that they are being judged by peers and professors. Grassian and Trueman wrote: "When students participate in a learning environment which is familiar and comfortable with online gaming, and virtual reality, they learn by exploring, by making mistakes and rectifying them, by coming up with creative and innovative solutions, and most importantly by putting theory into practice."[5] Second Life is an earlier iteration of technology used to create online virtual worlds, so the same principles apply to current VR programs.

The most laudable advantage is that VR allows for the transmission of knowledge without students feeling they are being preached at. Consequently, I am proposing using virtual reality to address the aforementioned issues. My project replaces the mundane, jargon-filled, lecture-based approach to instruction with dynamic, virtual reality modules consisting of familiar, recognizable, real-life simulated scenarios in order to make the learning objectives more easily comprehensible and improve student learning and retention. The following proverb sums up these issues perfectly: *"I hear, I forget. I see, I remember. I do, I understand."*

This VR project will elucidate for students that information literacy is not restricted to homework but is just as useful in their everyday life. Students are placed into realistic yet fantastically futuristic scenarios that highlight the confusing nature of discerning truth from falsehood. This project shows students that they inherently possess the cognitive tools to make necessary distinctions between fake or untrustworthy information and safer and more reasonable alternatives, in order to understand how to transfer their deductive reasoning skills to academic pursuits.

My guiding principle in creating this VR proposal is based on my belief that in order to achieve meaningful learning, students need to truly understand the real-world applications of their lessons. I posit that using real-life situations can make lessons easily identifiable and therefore more meaningful. Unfortunately, there is an increasing amount of fake news that is bombarding students on a daily basis. Fortunately, students already possess the intuitive capability to distinguish fake news from real news. My project uses actual examples of fake news scenarios taken from Snopes or stories circulating on the Internet, for students to evaluate. These are exercises based on familiar real-life scenarios. To allow for complexity, not all of the fake news scenarios have a clear-cut "true" or "false" correct answer. These mimic situations in real life that require nuanced critical assessments. I contend that we don't need to limit our instruction to antiquated lecture-based formats that are replete with unfamiliar jargon. Virtual reality affords us the opportunity to instead reveal to students the intuitive knowledge they already possess.

USER EXPERIENCE

I have devised many real-life scenarios in VR that are familiar to students, so they can choose wisely between the two scenarios they encounter. These scenarios do not require a lecture because the correct (safe) choice is pretty obvious. Here is just one example. Users are given the choice to identify the most trustworthy option when presented with two encounters, both involving strangers:

> **Option 1:** While you are on the dance floor, in a nightclub, a suspicious-looking stranger, whom you've never seen before, offers you a drink.

> **Option 2:** While you are in a hospital bed, surrounded by medical personnel, the Emergency Room (E.R.) Nurse, whom you've never met before, gives you water and pills.

The above are only two scenarios that illustrate the same "common-sense" thought processes that are used to evaluate the situations and determine who is a trusted source and ascribe a motive to each. This is the same skill needed to become information-literate. The suspicious stranger in the nightclub represents the same type of problems as does an unknown information provider, online. Conversely, the E.R. Nurse's credibility represents the trusted expertise of scholarly materials in academia.

After the nightclub level, students advance to different levels by flying through wormhole effects. On the next level, students have to make another wise choice and separate out real news reports from false accounts or fake news. Users move truthful items onto a 3D, free-floating, five-point star marked "True." Otherwise, they slide "Fake News" into a sunken, burning garbage bin, marked "Fake." The complexity results from the fact that there will be ambiguous virtual choices proffered, because in real life there are times when something is neither all true, nor all false.

Galileo stated it brilliantly: "You cannot teach a man anything; you can only help him to find it within himself."

LOGISTICS

Creating familiar real-life scenarios inside of virtual worlds is very expensive. I received estimates to bring my proposal to life ranging from $50,000 to $500,000. At these amounts, the project is cost-prohibitive, even after being scaled down using cost-saving measures provided by the developers. For example, one vendor proposed having product placement inside of the virtual world, on a billboard or in the nightclub. The idea is intriguing, but the library probably wouldn't allow sponsors using product placement inside of our virtual world.

More palatable cost-saving approaches were suggested by various vendors. One vendor suggested that creating 3D animated characters (e.g., the suspicious nightclub character) increases the price, but there are other creative ways to achieve the same desired experience of a choice between two strangers. Aside from the expense, having two completely different scenes would be wasteful and, from a "game play" point of view, slightly disjointed. A scenario that covered the presentation of both choices, but in a single setting, would be more efficient and cost-effective.

Another suggestion, reducing the quality or fidelity of the graphics in order to reduce cost is not an option. Producing low-quality imagery defeats the purpose of using immersive virtual reality technology. Instead, a more effective development alternative might be adjusting the "depth" of the experience. Depth refers to the increased variety or grandeur of environments: more elements in each scene, more depth of game-play. For example, using 360-degree video can be a cheaper option for the nightclub scenario. There could be cool animations that users can view by looking around.

Another cost-cutting measure is to simply have fewer backgrounds or scenario locations. There are cheaper alternatives such as using Google Cardboards with students' personal cellphones, instead of the more expensive Oculus Rift/HTC Vive headgear. My employer, Stanford University Libraries, could easily purchase fifteen Google Cardboard headsets to match the number of students in each mandatory library class. I was considering using Stanford students to build the VR experience. Unfortunately, using our students was not a viable option due to the constraints of our quarterly academic calendar.

There are other considerations besides the expense. The technology itself may have adverse effects on students who are sensitive to jerking movements in VR. Special consideration will be given to reducing the actions that contribute to users feeling discomfort while using the headgear. I was assured that careful design processes can eliminate elements that induce motion sickness or cause users to feel unwell. A few vendors encouraged incorporating hybrid reality or mixed reality components as a way to add variety, prevent motion sickness, and save money. Hybrid reality is a combination of animation and live-action features that merge to produce an environment in which users can interact with (real) physical as well as (virtual) digital objects.

"THE INFINITY LIBRARY"

The preceding sections have laid out my justification and overall concept for a virtual reality program. Below is an overview of the planning discussed with vendors in more detail. The first step in actual production is to create a Game Design Document (GDD). This is equivalent to creating a storyboard before producing a video. The VR setting will be dazzling, immersive, and futuristic. It is safe to assume that students will expect they are walking into a 3D version of the physical Stanford University Libraries, including a replica of the rows of stacks. But no! The setting will use distinctive details of the real library combined with magical realism. For marketing and branding purposes, the entrance to our fantasy world will be through a virtual replica of Stanford's iconic entrance and up the grand staircase.

When users ascend a re-creation of the grand staircase, this is where the simulation of the existing physical library ends, and an amazing new library world appears. Everything now looks different and the laws of physics don't apply. Corridors appear at impossible angles. The librarian materializes in the form of a floating, pulsating, glowing orb that is not in humanoid form but rather in the shape of a Librarian-Bot. The Librarian-Bot's function is to explain the goals and instructions for each scenario. The Librarian-Bot welcomes users to the Infinity Library, where all possibilities can happen, and where you must be the judge of what you see. This imagery encourages users to question everything they see, to get them into the correct frame of mind for the coming challenges or scenario. It will also elucidate the fact that inside of the Infinity Library, *the impossible is possible,* and this library does not operate at all like its real-world counterpart.

The Librarian-Bot guides users through the choices available and the reflection components, after each selection is made. The Librarian-Bot gauges the user's reactions and ascertains how the user felt about the experience, in real time. Reflection components ensure that the desired lesson was learned. If the reflection result was not satisfactory, there can be additional prompts to make the point more clearly. Based on user feedback, we can dynamically make the situations more difficult by changing preset variables. Alternatively, if users are struggling, we can reduce the complexity level.

The Librarian-Bot projects holographic images that transport users into each module. Users navigate through a simple-choice user interface (UI) that requires them to "choose wisely" from among different scenarios. Users travel through cool "wormhole" transition effects as scenarios move back and forth between the library and the information universe.

Students are free to fly, literally and metaphorically, since in virtual reality the laws of the physical world don't apply. The modules guide users through action-oriented and process-driven prompts. Users need to successfully complete each module in order to advance to the next level. Students will receive rewards for correct answers, as opposed to being penalized for incorrect ones. If designed correctly, the exercise should be enjoyable as well as educational.

A large part of overall assessment will include the innovation and uniqueness of this project. A literature review illustrated that no library has even attempted to experiment with using these immersive virtual reality technologies in instruction. This is just one aspect that makes this project so groundbreaking. I've had prior success managing a similar virtual reality project for library instruction, using Second Life, on the University of Notre Dame's private island, called Sophia. In my book *Cybrarian Extraordinaire,* I detail the specific activities as well as student assessments for this project. Archival video footage of my Second Life activities is on YouTube. The Scholarly versus Popular Journal Rack activity is titled "Sophia's Last Day—Part 7," and the Maze is titled "Sophia's Last Day—Part 5."

A 2014 article reported that more and more time and money are being devoted to teaching with virtual reality for students as early as kindergarten up through college.[6] Therefore, many K–12 students are being exposed to VR in classes, so by the time they are in college they will expect that same level of interactive instruction using virtual reality technology. The future is now.

Very soon, virtual reality will be an important instrument in any instructional tool chest. The library should be in the vanguard of this eventuality. This type of VR instructional undertaking has never been tried in librarianship for information literacy classes. Stanford University is in Silicon Valley, and people expect us to be educational trailblazers. This radically visionary project will create a truly avant-garde approach that catapults us into the virtual and eventual Future of Libraries.

Stanford already houses an innovative Virtual Human Interaction Lab (VHIL). Notably, one of their project areas is "Learning in Immersive VR." In 2017, Stanford began a strategic long-range planning process across the entire campus. This proposal was one of more than 2,800 ideas and proposals for Stanford's future that were submitted by members of the university community. The university announced that the proposals would be separated into white papers based on their overarching themes. There were four steering groups tasked with consolidating the proposals submitted to the university. On February 23, 2018, the Education Steering Group presented to the Faculty Senate and explained that they are focused on fostering innovation in the classroom. "Many of the proposals challenge Stanford to be a world leader in understanding the best ways for learning to happen." The group stated, "In order to do that, we have to take some bold steps and think differently about our educational program." My virtual reality proposal is definitely bold and is obviously a different way of thinking about education. Most importantly, this project will demonstrate a groundbreaking approach to instruction; these increasingly ubiquitous technologies are waiting to be explored by bold visionaries, who are the vanguard of the teaching profession.

CONCLUSION

My main approach to instruction is to help students realize that they already have the knowledge and basic skills needed for research inside of them. In my classes, I explain that a database or catalog is just another website. They acknowledge using websites every day, sometimes all day! They successfully navigate new websites, usually without taking a class on how to use that new website. They just figure it out, because they intuitively understand how to process new information that they encounter. I firmly contend that the instructor's role is simply to enlighten learners that they already possess the basic skills needed for research.

> I never teach my pupils. I only attempt to provide the conditions in which they can learn. —Albert Einstein

I agree wholeheartedly with Einstein: I consider myself to be a sanguine guide for novice travelers, and I accompany them on their information-seeking journey until they are sufficiently research-enlightened and prepared to continue, alone, on their path to becoming lifelong knowledge seekers. I empower them with the tools to enable them to make the Unknown, "*Known.*"

In closing, I would like to draw a parallel to the scene in the movie the *Wizard of Oz* when Dorothy misses her balloon ride home; she is utterly distraught and cries out of fear that she will never get where she is trying to go. It is at this point that Glinda, the Good Witch, highlights the fact that with her ruby red slippers, Dorothy has had the power to go home the whole time. Dorothy just needed to discover this power for herself. The moral being, whenever they are in doubt, they can simply look within themselves for the answers. We are more powerful than we think. This is the same overarching message to those travelers on the path to information literacy enlightenment: "Look within for your power of critical evaluation."

So, in applying this self-discovery concept to my virtual reality program:

- Dorothy represents the patron.
- Glinda the Good Witch represents the librarian, naturally.
- The hot-air balloon represents traditional classroom lecture workshops.
- And the ruby slippers represent the "common sense" that the patrons have had all along.

The librarian simply needs to point this out to the patrons, so that they finally understand that they could have been information-literate this entire time, even without the traditional classroom workshops. As students explore the information universe, they need only look within themselves for the answers they seek about critical evaluation. It is our job, as librarians, to guide them to the knowledge that they are more powerful than they think, not just in virtual reality but also in real life.

NOTES

1. Sara Rimer, "At MIT, Large Lectures Are Going the Way of the Blackboard," *New York Times,* January 12, 2009, https://www.nytimes.com/2009/01/13/us/13physics.html.
2. Rimer, "At MIT."
3. Sue Schallenbarger, "Most Students Don't Know When News Is Fake, Stanford Study Finds," *Wall Street Journal,* November 21, 2016.
4. Zahira Merchant et al., "Effectiveness of Virtual Reality-Based Instruction on Students' Learning Outcomes in K-12 and Higher Education: A Meta-Analysis," *Computers & Education* 70 (2014): 31.
5. Esther Grassian and Rhonda Trueman, "Stumbling, Bumbling, Teleporting and Flying . . . Librarian Avatars in Second Life," *Reference Services Review* 35, no. 1 (2007): 84–89, https://doi.org/10.1108/00907320710729382.
6. Merchant et al., "Effectiveness," 36.

BIBLIOGRAPHY

Condic, Kristine. "Using Second Life as a Training Tool in an Academic Library." *The Reference Librarian* 50, no. 4 (2009): 333–45.

Freeman, S., S. L. Eddy, M. McDonough, M. K. Smith, N. Okoroafor, H. Jordt, and M. P. Wenderoth. "Active Learning Increases Student Performance in Science, Engineering, and Mathematics." *Proceedings of the National Academy of Sciences of the United States of America* 111, no. 23 (June 10, 2014): 8410–15.

Grassian, Esther, and Rhonda Trueman. "Stumbling, Bumbling, Teleporting and Flying . . . Librarian Avatars in Second Life." *Reference Services Review* 35, no. 1 (2007): 84–89. doi:10.1108/00907320710729382.

Merchant, Zahira, Ernest T. Goetz, Lauren Cifuentes, Wendy Keeney-Kennicutt, and Trina J. Davis. "Effectiveness of Virtual Reality-Based Instruction on Students' Learning Outcomes in K-12 and Higher Education: A Meta-Analysis." *Computers & Education* 70 (2014): 29–40.

Rimer, Sara. "At MIT, Large Lectures Are Going the Way of the Blackboard." *New York Times*, January 12, 2009. https://www.nytimes.com/2009/01/13/us/13physics .html.

Santos, Jonathan Faustino, and Sharon Maria Esposo-Betan. "Advantages and Challenges of Using Augmented Reality for Library Orientations in an Academic/ Research Library Setting." Proceedings of the IATUL Conferences. Paper 7. https://docs.lib.purdue.edu/iatul/2017/challenges/7/.

Shellenbarger, Sue. "Most Students Don't Know When News Is Fake, Stanford Study Finds." *Wall Street Journal*, November 21, 2016, Life & Arts section.

BRIGITTE BELL and
TERRY COTTRELL

8

Augmented Reality in the Library

Pivoting toward a Security-First
Implementation Strategy

PREDICTIONS THAT AUGMENTED REALITY WOULD BECOME A
library technology to be reckoned with have proven true. Now that successful
models for implementation have been established, libraries can more easily
decide if and how they want to invest in AR technology, depending on their
price point, the needs of their user base, and increasingly, with considerations
about identifying cybersecurity threats. As AR technologies have developed
and become more widespread, serious ethical, safety, and even health considerations have come into focus, with the interaction between library users and
AR content front and center. This interaction has shifted from being purely
focused on innovative experiences and new windows to discovery toward an
inextricable hybrid involving information privacy, safety, and security. The
question is: is there a clear dichotomy present between security and access
to AR technology, or can there be a happy medium? We argue that a middle
ground is desirable, but there will likely need to be a balance between security and access, perhaps with more emphasis on preventing attacks than on
enabling unfettered user access going forward. This chapter will discuss how
libraries can offer AR experiences to their users while also ensuring that users'
privacy and security are adequately protected.

AUGMENTED REALITY IN THE LIBRARY
Past and Present

AR technologies have played a significant role in taking libraries from simple facilities where users can access materials, to transforming them into innovative spaces with a capacity for dynamic interactions and experiences. While libraries have traditionally sought to bring users into spaces for exploration and education via curated resources that enable self-discovery and self-visualization, AR library implementations encourage users to utilize materials that blend self-discovery with visualization that is less dependent on the user's imagination. AR visitations are not only presented to users, but are so immersive as to completely take over the senses and provide an experience like no other in human history. In no uncertain terms, AR technologies have been a game changer for libraries, and the manifestations of this are as unique and diverse as libraries themselves.

The closest historical library technologies that have offered users a type of augmented reality are the presentation of scanned documents within databases. Even older microfilm and microfiche media offered a taste of what the original "real" information product looked like without simulating how print media feels in the hands of the user. The advantage of these older technologies included (at the time) the ability to store large amounts of information in much smaller physical spaces, of course. The ability to satisfy quick retrieval, however, is something that had always been present in the library user's mind before Internet technology came along to match the desire. The development of whole-Internet searching, proliferated by Google's algorithms, delivered fully on this need by giving users the power to simultaneously search multiple information sources, in a process akin to looking down multiple rows of bookshelves (and being able to read all titles and authors) all at once instead of being required to look down each shelf one row and one title at a time.

The development of the database as an augmented version of a file cabinet is ultimately what unleashed information access to the point where users are now unaware of how their access has been magnified well past the point of past methods of searching; they do not truly know how big the "file cabinets" are in size today. Most users are uncaring in this sense; they simply want to "feel" as if they have full abilities to search instantaneously, whether this feeling stems from a real experience or not. For example, the existence and growth of the deep web are not known to most users of the Internet at large.[1] Users have been trained, or they unknowingly train themselves, to accept popular search engine results as true total results from the entire Internet, while never asking, "Am I experiencing all there is on the Web? What am I not finding by using the single interface of Google or Bing?" Library users can physically walk the entire stacks of a building, footprinting the entire space to get a true understanding of just how much information is within their reach. With the advent of databases, however, information seekers have limited abilities to gauge the scope of the information that is within their grasp. Without this ability to footprint the Internet, and its dark web, users are presented with a different version of reality, depending on their skill set and their level of technical training with computer networks.

More astute information-seeking users have turned to the TOR Browser for access to deep web content. Having more awareness of just how big the data sinks are that drive AR technologies does, in fact, give a distinct few an advantage over the many. With the advent of cybersecurity training from the Department of Homeland Security's National Initiative for Cybersecurity Careers and Studies, numerous traditional university programs, the SANS Institute, the EC-Council and others, knowledge of the dark web and overall understanding of how the Internet works and serves information to a variety of network types via all means—with AR being one of the most advanced— is growing steadily. This movement does not exempt libraries, but rather automatically included them after the 9–11 terror attacks, when libraries made changes to the retention of patron borrowing records in an attempt to increase privacy and protect users' experiences with information materials. Once libraries began to take action in this realm, they took an important step as a precursor to information security, Internet privacy and identity management in both the real and virtual worlds at large. AR technologies have yet to truly solve the problem that libraries first confronted seventeen years ago: how can users' identity and information-seeking activities be made private so as to lessen the ability of a third party to create (or steal) a virtual identity from an individual or group within a given AR system? Physical library users can rest assured that their physical activities within libraries are secure to a degree that was not yet planned for when AR technologies are adopted as an exciting means of opening doors to new aspects of information discovery.

PUBLIC LIBRARIES
Augmented Reality as a Gateway to New Experiences

Public libraries can now offer their patrons an immersive experience like no other by showcasing wearable AR technologies like Oculus Rift. In the public library sphere, users vary the most in terms of access and their ability to pragmatically integrate AR into their lives. Some public library patrons can afford to purchase AR tools and technologies, and they are expecting more and more opportunities to use their mobile phones and tablets as part of their everyday experience. Airports and train stations provide quick charging stations for phones, laptops, and tablets. Movie theaters and concert venues offer options to purchase and scan tickets via mobile devices. More affluent library users accustomed to these types of services will come to expect similar offerings in their public library spaces.

For other public library users, virtual technologies like AR are much more of a novelty. These users have little or no idea that AR technologies exist, or that their libraries can introduce users to a new world of information that aims to use the physical world as a catalyst for the virtual. More and more, public libraries are expected to keep pace with the external market in offering their users exciting and immersive experiences through innovative new forms of technology. With new AR integration in public libraries, these same users will come into their library for a familiar purpose and walk out with a new understanding of what is possible, because their library will lead them on the way to embracing this paradigm shift. Indeed, while the variety of possibilities is infinite on the patron side within public libraries, the need to integrate AR in every public library is becoming more apparent and clear.

Are these technologies absolutely safe for users? What are the risks? Institutions that are considering AR implementations like Oculus or devices from other providers risk exposing individuals to the triggering of latent phobias related to heights or sounds. Seizure risk is ever-present, as are injuries due to blackouts and dizziness.[2] Head-mounted displays have been empirically shown to negatively affect the stable posture abilities of older adults with balance problems.[3] No AR system currently exists that is being robustly assessed for its psychological benefits or detriment. What if users become "addicted" to AR implementations? How much time should an individual allot for each daily use? Should these limits be set by age range as well? Best practices are yet to be established.

ACADEMIC LIBRARIES
Augmented Reality in Research and Discovery

Based on the high percentage of their clientele utilizing mobile devices, academic libraries' strategies for serving the needs of these highly tech-equipped individuals are inherently different from those of public libraries. Most college students carry at least one mobile device that is capable of basic AR interaction. Academic library users will view many of the AR-related activities and offerings at their public libraries as more appropriate for leisure time activities. When they encounter AR at their university, they expect something different—technology that is both entertaining and useful. The key for academic libraries is to find ways that AR applications can be customized in order to assist with learning and facilitate research and discovery.

Insofar as AR is very helpful with finding desired locations (e.g., restaurants, clubs, parks), it is inherently centered on discovery. This is where the tie to academic research begins. Academic libraries' focus on the need for faculty and students to "discover" information is how strategies for implementation can be successfully formed. There are many possible avenues for how this might be accomplished. Primarily, AR applications are useful to students in their ability to guide them to related content. AR applications also present an exciting new platform for multidimensional visualization projects, particularly at universities with robust programs in the natural sciences, architecture, engineering, pre-med, and nursing.

The harassment and bullying of students seen on college campuses can be replicated in AR environments, perhaps more rapidly and with a much higher degree of anonymity. Allowing anonymous users is therefore not advised. The same common cybersecurity threats that are present outside of AR systems, like injection flaws involving users attempting to execute unintended commands from systems, poor security configurations from technicians who initially install the systems and provide maintenance, and insufficient monitoring, can also occur within AR systems.[4] Presented separately, AR and cybersecurity took the main focus of attention at the Consumer Electronics Show (CES 2018) in Las Vegas, Nevada.[5] There is no reason to assume that these subjects will remain separate from one another, and still be so high in popularity. With most of the explosion of interest in AR and cybersecurity focused on the realm of mobile devices, and 28 percent of nearly 5 billion smartphones still without even a simple screen lock for security, and given the fact that a high percentage of college students use the devices each day, academic libraries face a troubling future filled with many concerns related to potential AR security risks at every turn.[6]

SPECIAL LIBRARIES
Augmented Reality's Role in Elevating Special Collections

Special libraries are in the most unique position with AR in that their user base is highly targeted and generally narrower in focus in terms of users' needs and preferences. For the purposes of this section, it is important to focus specifically on special libraries that are their own separate entities, rather than special libraries affiliated or housed within larger academic libraries, since these often tend to take on the characteristics of the academic libraries themselves. Because of their size, these small special libraries often face limited resources as well as considerable budgetary restrictions. Approaching the board of directors of a small special library with numerous examples and case studies is the very best place to begin work in utilizing AR in the institution.

If special library administrators are interested in experimenting, there are many freely available AR apps and development platforms. Location-based apps are particularly useful because they can be used to create virtual walking tours that will highlight historically significant objects and locations or specific items within special library collections. Hiring an intern to develop the content for the information is a good way to bridge the funding gap between needing to test the usefulness of AR tools and not having the financial support to restructure a staff position to specifically target this still mostly underutilized technology. If an AR visualization project is seen as a promising addition to a collection (in the case of museum and archives libraries), consulting and visiting with other institutions that can demonstrate their current implementations is advised as a way to be successful right from the start.

PRACTICAL CONSIDERATIONS
Access, Privacy, and Security

Our previous chapter on this subject focused on budget and cost-effectiveness as primary metrics for whether libraries should choose to invest in AR technologies.[7] While these financial concerns are still highly relevant, the recent growth and expansion of AR has led to an all-new set of concerns—privacy and security chief among them. As with any Internet-supported technology, concerns regarding privacy and ethical use are at the forefront.

Security concerns in regard to AR primarily revolve around the collection of user data. An individual user's eye movements, body language, heart rate, and emotional responses can all be recorded using AR technologies.[8] How and to what extent should this be data collected, and to what end? VR technologies also often record users' exact locations and personal contact information, as well as stored payment methods such as bank account and credit card numbers. Were there to be any sort of data breach, users of these technologies could be made extremely vulnerable. Mary Lynne Nielsen, the global operations and outreach program director for the Institute of Electrical and Electronics Engineers Standards Association, has addressed additional concerns in regard to the manner in which content is ultimately delivered.[9] Aside from the obvious concerns regarding how users' private information is collected, used, and stored, serious ethical considerations can and should be raised in regard to how targeted information is overlaid on top of reality interfaces. Who has the final say over what is included in this content, how it is delivered, and who its target audience is?

AN EXAMPLE OF SUCCESSFUL IMPLEMENTATION
Pulseworks

A provider of one of the more forward-thinking and advanced product line offerings, Pulseworks is a company which offers custom augmented reality simulation stations. It provides five standard offerings: (1) a virtual reality transporter that combines 360-degree content with users wearing a headset sitting in a seat on a movable platform, (2) a fully immersive 360-degree flight simulator, (3) a capsule that up to 20 users can enter, and which combines motion 3D and 4D motion content, (4) a smaller 8-seat capsule version for smaller installations, and (5) a 2-seat submarine edition specifically for undersea simulations. Installed at the Field Museum of Natural History in Chicago, the VR transporter platform requires users to sit in a chair wearing an augmented reality headset, but it provides a full range of motion for the head and neck. This enables patrons to view content in any direction while the seat platform moves underneath to simulate activities shown within the view screens.

Users can also still communicate orally with one another, allowing them to experience greater AR while sitting next to each other.

Installed at the St. Louis Science Center, the 360-degree flight simulator model is built to real airplane specifications, with cockpit seats and a manual sliding entry door; it simulates 360-degree barrel rolls, and seats a pilot and copilot. Users view content on a screen in place of the cockpit front window. The system can be designed to simulate a variety of real-world airplane designs. All aspects of flight simulation are integrated in the installation, and the system uses 500 watts of digital surround sound to simulate real airplane experiences. The twenty-seat capsule AR simulation module (called the Morphis) is designed for larger crowds. The content for this system focuses on educational material, virtual worlds, and adventure stories. Driven by a three-axis hydraulic system, much more of the AR experience for users comes from physical sensations, in addition to what is projected onto the eyes and broadcast to the ears. The Morphis can be found in the Smithsonian National Air and Space Museum–Steven F. Udvar-Hazy Center, National Museum of American History, Oregon Museum of Science and Industry, Space Center Houston, National Museum of the United States Air Force, Toronto Zoo, Audubon Zoo, Cleveland Zoo, Broadway at the Beach, and Pacific Science Center.[10] The system is safe for outdoor installations, and it uses rear-projection and multi-channel surround sound.

A smaller, eight-seat version of the Morphis provides a similar experience to the larger capsule module, but it has less impact on a budget. It has a much lower installation height requirement, so it will fit in smaller spaces. Eighty riders per hour can safely use the system. Instead of hydraulic movement, the smaller Morphis ESP uses all-electric motion, a similar display to that of the 360-degree flight simulator model. Finally, the submarine-based simulator edition encourages participants to work together as a team to solve an undersea mystery by using navigation skills and collecting DNA samples. Even 360-degree rolls are achievable with this model, like the flight simulator product. Other product specifications present in the flight simulator are used in this submarine model as well. The recommended run time for each user is shorter, however, at five minutes. Overall, more than twenty minutes in any of the Pulseworks products is not recommended, because unexpected disorientation and loss of unconscious stability control for the neck and eyes could lead to temporary dizziness. No personal user information is collected from users of any of Pulseworks systems at this time, but it can be assumed that as the popularity of these AR experiences continues to grow, the ability to link user personal information for off-site engagement with content (especially through social media accounts) will be a desired connection for Pulseworks to try to integrate into its products, as a way to keep patrons engaged once they exit one of the installations.

LOOKING AHEAD
Predictions, Recommendations, Conclusions

It is fair to say that libraries in general place a higher priority on user privacy as an ethical imperative. When making decisions regarding which type of AR technology to invest in, libraries should consider options that align with their current policies, particularly policies regarding technology and user privacy. As with any online application platform, augmented reality raises issues regarding the collection of users' personal information without their expressed consent. While the majority of mobile applications primarily seek to analyze hardware utilization and Internet connectivity, legal regulations in place to prevent these applications from accessing a user's personal information are currently lacking.[11] A recent Pew Research study indicates that a majority of users in the United States have serious concerns regarding their privacy on mobile devices.[12] Library administrators should take these concerns seriously and should perform due diligence to ensure that their users' privacy and security is in no way undermined by their use of these innovative—and occasionally controversial—technologies. With the variety of examples of successful implementation of AR technology now in place, the library community can begin moving towards a working model of how these types of resources can best be incorporated into their resources. Libraries of all shapes and sizes are embracing their roots as places where users can go to experience new and different ways to learn and discover. If libraries can continue finding ways to balance innovation and creativity with fiscal responsibility and a balance between the myriad of ways to discover and learn, AR technologies will undoubtedly continue to play a critical role within the progress of information discovery and the value of libraries within their communities.

How can libraries better ensure comprehensive physical and cyber security for their AR users? One way is through the testing and vetting of the physical security issues related to AR hardware use. Another method involves being conscious of how users access content in these systems, and advising users of potential compromises to personal data related to using their credentials from an outside system within an AR installation. One way AR system designers have attempted to heighten security for users is the employment of 3D passwords where users must recall a complex set of actions performed within an AR environment in order to gain access (e.g., the password to access a system is only achieved when a user enters a particular virtual garage and sits in a particular car of a particular color). Many users, however, may not be able to interpret how to use a 3D password system, because they are so accustomed to PIN-based and pattern-based passwords adopted from the operating systems of their own personal mobile devices.[13] One specific technology used to accomplish this with AR technologies, 3DPass, has been shown to have a much higher memorability rate versus traditional password strategies currently in use outside of the AR world.[14] Traditional passwords are said to be made more secure through the use of multifactor authentication, and even through the use of physical hardware key supplementation from vendors like RSA or Yubikey.[15] 3D passwords, however, require users to replicate all the specific steps of a previous experience they had within the virtual world they are attempting to reenter after logging off. This password methodology may offer users a level of security authentication that is much more improbable for an attacker to guess, mimic, or compromise, depending on the level of detail required by the 3D password system.

In the end, AR may well become the preferred reality for users of information resource content that has moved from paper to screen, from storage shelves to databases, from interaction with eyes and ears only to full sensory immersion. Whether for research or entertainment purposes, the appeal of AR for libraries is the promise of mixing business with pleasure. The popularity of AR systems (as the world has seen with the explosion of online social networks that have enriched their host companies to the point of placing their executives at the tables of the World Economic Forum, and have amassed more users than many entire countries have citizens) will drive more legitimate agents looking to provide information, but also potentially more malicious agents who are trying to phish for damage or dox unsuspecting victims for financial gain.[16] Combined with physical health concerns from the overuse of AR systems, the cause for concern is clear. Library administrators who pivot toward AR implementations with a focus on both physical and cybersecurity for their patrons will enjoy more of the positive promises of the technologies with minimal threats, lawsuits, and headaches. Regardless, the appeal of AR means the demand from users is coming, and the budgetary support and will of constituents need to match future desires. The appeal of AR's speed, sensory immersion, and its potential to present informative content in a delightful way with sounds, colors, and moving content in ways unparalleled in human history is invading the consumer space in a way that will force libraries to adapt and acquiesce to a variety of integrations into their existing spaces and program offerings going forward.

NOTES

1. Jose Pagliery, "The Deep Web You Don't Know About," CNN, last modified March 10, 2014, http://money.cnn.com/2014/03/10/technology/deep-web/index.html.
2. Maria Korolov, "The Real Risks of Virtual Reality," *Risk Management* 61, no. 8 (2014): 20–24.
3. Paula Epure et al., "The Effect of Oculus Rift HMD on Postural Stability," Proceedings of the 10th International Conference on Disability Virtual Reality and Associated Technologies, 2014.
4. "Top 10—2017," Open Web Application Security Project, last modified March 27, 2018, https://www.owasp.org/index.php/Top_10-2017_Top_10.

5. Joshua Meredith, "Augmented Reality and Cybersecurity Will Headline 2018's CES," Georgetown School of Continuing Studies, last modified November 9, 2017, https://scs.georgetown.edu/news-and-events/article/6924/augmented-reality-and-cybersecurity-will-headline-2018s-ces.

6. Lee Rainie, "10 Facts about Smartphones as the iPhone Turns 10," Pew Research Center, last modified June 28, 2017, www.pewresearch.org/fact-tank/2017/06/28/10-facts-about-smartphones/.

7. Brigitte Bell and Terry Cottrell, "Hands-Free Augmented Reality: Impacting the Library Future," in *The Top Technologies Every Librarian Needs to Know: A LITA Guide,* ed. Kenneth J. Varnum (Chicago: American Library Association, 2014).

8. Tim Sparapani, "Can We Have Our Virtual Reality Cake and Eat It Too?" *Forbes,* last modified August 16, 2017, https://www.forbes.com/sites/timsparapani/2017/08/16/can-we-have-our-virtual-reality-cake-and-eat-it-too/ #22f082145369.

9. Mary Lynne Nielsen, "Augmented Reality and Its Impact on the Internet, Security, and Privacy," Beyond Standards (IEEE Standards Association), last modified July 10, 2015, https://beyond standards.ieee.org/augmented-reality/augmented-reality-and-its-impact-on-the-internet-security-and-privacy/.

10. "Morphis Motion Theatre Capsule Simulator," Pulseworks Web, last modified 2018, https://www.pulseworks.com/products/morphis-motion-theater-capsule-simulator.

11. Matthew Hettrich, "Data Privacy Regulation in the Age of Smartphones," *Touro Law Review* 31, no. 4 (2015): 17.

12. Monica Anderson, "Key Takeaways on Mobile Apps and Privacy," Pew Research Center, last modified November 10, 2015, www.pewresearch.org/fact-tank/2015/11/10/key-takeaways-mobile-apps/.

13. Zhen Yu et al., "An Exploration of Usable Authentication Mechanisms for Virtual Reality Systems," paper presented at Circuits and Systems (APCCAS): The 2016 IEEE Asia Pacific Conference, 2016.

14. Jonathan Gurary, Ye Zhu, and Huirong Fu, "Leveraging 3D Benefits for Authentication," *International Journal of Communications, Network and System Sciences* no. 8 (2017): 324.

15. Robert Künnemann and Graham Steel. "YubiSecure? Formal Security Analysis Results for the Yubikey and YubiHSM." *Revised Selected Papers of the 8th Workshop on Security and Trust Management,* 2012.

16. "Facebook Bigger Than 3 of the World's Biggest Countries," CBS News, last modified June 27, 2017, https://www.cbsnews.com/news/facebook-users-2-billion-biggest-countries/.

MICHAEL RIESEN

9
Augmented Reality and Virtual Reality and Their Legal Implications for Libraries

LIBRARIES, AND THE SERVICES OFFERED THROUGH LIBRARIES, must adhere to laws that address the legal rights associated with copyrights, patents, and trademarks, as well as federal and state laws relating to an individual's right of privacy and data protection. These are collectively known as "intellectual property laws." In this chapter, we will explore the ever-increasing use of technology by libraries, namely in the areas of augmented reality and virtual reality experiences, and identify potential issues that a library may encounter—and the rights a library may leverage—when it expands its services to include AR/VR experiences.[1]

COPYRIGHT

Copyright law grants the author of an original work a bundle of exclusive rights to decide how that work may be used by others.[2] Types of original works that may be protected by copyright include software, video games, and AR/VR programs and content, for example. The exclusive rights in the copyrighted work include the right to reproduce the work, to prepare additional works based on or derived from the original work, and to distribute copies. Importantly, the author's exclusive rights in the work may be transferred to other individuals or entities. As discussed herein, the mechanism for such transfers (for example, assignment, exclusive license agreement, nonexclusive license agreement) becomes an important inquiry for a library in managing its potential liability under copyright law.

When someone copies a copyrighted work without permission, the copyright holder may sue for infringement. To assert a claim of copyright infringement in court, the copyright owner must demonstrate "(1) ownership of a valid copyright, and (2) copying of constituent elements of the work that are original."[3] Proving the first element—ownership of a valid copyright—requires evidence of "(1) originality in the author; (2) copyrightability of the subject matter; (3) a national point of attachment of the work, such as to permit a claim of copyright; (4) compliance with applicable statutory formalities; and (5) (if the plaintiff is not the author) a transfer of rights or other relationship between the author and the plaintiff so as to constitute the plaintiff as the valid copyright claimant."[4] Proving the second element—copying of the constituent elements of the work that are original—requires evidence of (1) access to the copyrighted work, and (2) similarities between the copyrighted work and the allegedly infringing work.

In the context of AR/VR, the technology stack offers many layers of copyrightable works. For example, the code defining the operating system of the hardware used may be protected by copyright. As a further example, the elements of a user interface or the underlying source code defining a software application that is used to deliver the AR/VR experience may be protected by copyright. As yet a further example, the content provided in the AR/VR experience as a virtual audio or visual work may be protected by copyright. Therefore, when offering an AR/VR experience as part of library services, the library must first understand the full scope of the potential copyright protection involved—from the platform, to the content displayed, to the end-user, and every layer in between.

Historically, copyright laws and court decisions interpreting those laws guided libraries on how to use copyrighted works without infringing a holder's exclusive rights. As an example, the Copyright Act of 1976 is a United States law that includes multiple provisions defining the rights of copyright holders. The first sale doctrine is a provision in the Copyright Act which provides that an individual who lawfully purchases a copy of a copyrighted work may sell it, rent it, give it away, display it, or destroy it without infringing the copyright holder's rights.[5] As such, the purchaser of a copyrighted work receives certain legal rights on how that copyrighted work may be used in the future, such as lending the work to patrons of a library.

But how have these legal constructs been applied in the technologically advancing world of the library sciences? For starters, the rights afforded by the first sale doctrine do not "extend to any person who has acquired possession of the copy or phonorecord from the copyright owner, by rental, lease, loan, or otherwise, without acquiring ownership of it."[6] Said another way, the bundle of rights an individual may acquire in a copyrighted work turns on how such copyrighted work was conveyed. Many software- or computer-implemented works are provided under a license agreement rather than a purchase. Under a license agreement, the copyright holder remains the "owner" of the work and the distributed copies, but grants permission to the licensee to use the work for a particular purpose. As such, obtaining copies or distributing derivative works initially obtained under a license agreement may not afford the safeguards provided by the first sale doctrine.[7] Therefore, it is imperative that a library consider the means by which it is acquiring a copyrighted work— whether the transfer is a sale, or something less than a full transfer of the bundle of rights.

The same legal principles apply in AR/VR. But in these particular technologies, there may be multiple layers of copyrighted works to consider. For the discussion in this chapter, we will assume three categories of the parties involved in providing an AR/VR service at your institution:

1. Author/creator
2. Curator/operator
3. End user

Author/creator: The author, creator, or developer of a work is often the copyright owner. However, contracts such as employment agreements, work for hire agreements, or development agreements may contractually define copyright ownership. With regard to software and content development, as discussed herein, each entity (e.g., a library) is encouraged to revisit employment agreements, independent contractor agreements, and development agreements, among others, to ensure that the resultant ownership of copyrightable works is defined in the manner contemplated by the parties involved.

In the context of AR/VR, there may be several distinct "creators" that facilitate the full AR/VR experience. Consider, first, the AR/VR hardware device. Whether the AR/VR device is a headset, glasses, or a software application executing on an end user's smart device, software controls the operation of the device. And the source code of the operating system and coded application running via the operating system has creators. When you purchase the AR/VR headset, it is important to understand whether the software necessary to operate the functions of the headset is provided under a sale or is somehow licensed separately.[8] Here, the management of copyrighted works that are part of the AR/VR device may best be handled through negotiated agreement(s) with the copyright holders. But it is important to ensure that the contemplated agreement is with the copyright holder and that the party to the agreement has the authority that they claim to possess.

In another instance, the creator may be the developer of a software application that is used to provide the AR experience. In this instance, the library system may develop its own proprietary application and thus may become the copyright holder in the application itself. Or the library system may partner with a third-party developer having an existing AR/VR platform. Whether the library system decides to jointly develop an application or to use a complete platform from a third party, it is important to ensure that the agreements address the ownership of the copyrighted works and the definition of what use rights are explicitly transferred to the library system.

In yet another example, the creator may be the author of the content that is displayed to an end user in the AR/VR experience. The content may be original and may itself be subject to protection under the copyright laws. However, some may argue that the content in an AR or VR experience is derivative from copyrighted works in the real world. Take, for example, an AR overlay of content on a page of a book, a painting, or an architectural work. One must ask whether the underlying, real-world work is protected by copyright or whether it is in the public domain. If the underlying work is protected by copyright, then the AR content overlaying the real-world work may be considered a derivative work and may then require permission from the copyright holder in the underlying work. This derivative work example is demonstrative of the new legal issues that have not yet been expressly defined in the law.

Curator/operator: The curators may be considered a middle entity between the creators and the end users. It is contemplated herein that the library may take on the role of the curator or operator in the AR/VR domain. In this role, the library may be responsible for acquiring or at least promoting the platform to host the AR/VR experience. Moreover, the curator may be responsible for developing, acquiring, or coordinating the content that will be provided to the end users in the AR/VR experience. Again, if the library creates original content for the AR/VR experience, it may be the copyright owner. As an example, a library may develop a proprietary application with original content and may be the copyright owner of the works developed therein. However, it is likely that content provided in an AR/VR experience may be created by parties outside the library system. Thus, the curator must acquire the rights to use the content in the AR/VR experience. We reference again the distinction between purchasing the content and licensing the content for a prescribed use. Such a distinction in how the content is "acquired" may be clearly defined in the agreement between the curator and the author of the content.

Alternatively, a curator may adopt the role of a service provider. Laws such as the Digital Millennium Copyright Act (DMCA) include safe harbor provisions for a "service provider." Under the DMCA, a service provider must lack knowledge of the infringement of a user, cannot receive a financial benefit from the infringing activity, cannot have the ability to control the infringing activity, and upon notification the service provider must remove or disable access to the infringing content. Although these provisions are relied on in the context of Internet service providers and those hosting web pages for users, in the context of AR/VR, the service provider role is not as clear. The DMCA gives two definitions for the phrase "service provider":

> (A) As used in subsection (a), the term "service provider" means an entity offering the transmission, routing, or providing of connections for digital online communications, between or among points specified by a user, of material of the user's choosing, without modification to the content of the material as sent or received.

> (B) As used in this section, other than in subsection (a), the term "service provider" means a provider of online services or network access, or the operator of facilities therefor, and includes an entity described in subparagraph (A).[9]

Therefore, in order for a library to fit the definition of a "service provider" under the DMCA and to garner the protections provided in the safe harbor provisions, the library must not take an active role in the creation, presentation, and modification of content in the AR/VR experience. Instead, the library must simply be a conduit of the information between the creator and the end users.

Since new AR/VR content and the means for adapting such content are being developed on a daily basis, it is unclear whether the current laws and related safe harbors are sufficient to address the unique nature of the AR/VR experience.

End user: An end user may be a patron of the library system who engages in the AR/VR experience. The unique environment of an AR/VR experience puts the end user in control of the presentation of content—that is, copyrighted works. For example, the user may need to look at a particular place or may need to engage in certain activities to trigger content to be presented. This action alone complicates the legal analysis of potential copyright infringement and the defenses to such infringement. To further complicate such issues, many AR/VR experiences have the capability to present custom content based on the end user's interactions with the experience. End-user inputs such as location, point of view, and user preferences or filters, for example, may be used to alter the content that is presented to a particular end user or the manner in which such content is presented. Thus, the end user's action may create an instance of potential copyright infringement, but evidencing the same may require procedures that are not fully contemplated by current laws and rules governing the enforcement of copyright infringement. Moreover, a copyright holder may seek remedies for the infringing acts of an end user by making a claim against the curator/operator or the developer. Again, such risk must be mitigated through an understanding of the copyright stack in the AR/VR experience and the agreements between all of the parties.

What about an affirmative defense of fair use? Fair use is an affirmative defense that permits the unlicensed use of copyrighted works in certain circumstances.[10] Such circumstances that may qualify as fair use include criticism, comment, news reporting, teaching, scholarship, and research.[11] But fair use is not an absolute defense, and the analysis of whether such unlicensed use of the copyrighted work is fair use is on a case-by-case basis. Some factors that may be considered are (1) the purpose of the use—commercial or nonprofit educational purposes; (2) the nature of the copyrighted work; (3) the amount and substantiality of the use in relation to the copyrighted work; and (4) the effect of the use upon the potential market for the copyrighted work. Universities and library systems have developed fair use guidelines to help manage risks in their educational use of copyrighted material. However, such guidelines are not dispositive of how a court will treat the use. Moreover, some of the education guidelines and policies adopted by educational entities do not contemplate the unique nature of the AR/VR experience. As with any of the preceding comments on copyright law, an entity such as a library that is preparing to host or develop an AR/VR experience should thoroughly consider the role that the library will play in delivering the AR/VR experience and the nature of the AR/VR service that is being offered.

TRADEMARKS

A trademark is a word, symbol, or phrase that is used to identify and distinguish one's goods from those manufactured or sold by others and to indicate the source of the goods.[12] A trademark owner may sue subsequent parties for infringing their trademark.[13] To prove infringement of a trademark, the trademark owner must show that there is a "likelihood of confusion" between the infringing use and the subject trademark. In particular, the use of a trademark in commerce may constitute infringement if such use is likely to cause consumer confusion as to the source or sponsorship of those goods. The U.S. courts have relied on several factors to help guide the analysis of trademark infringement. Those factors include (1) the strength of the mark; (2) the proximity of the goods; (3) the similarity of the marks; (4) evidence of actual confusion; (5) the similarity of marketing channels used; (6) the degree of caution exercised by the typical purchaser; and (7) the defendant's intent.[14]

When we consider AR/VR, determining trademark infringement based on the use of similar marks in a virtual environment is not as clear as in the physical world. Would a consumer likely be confused that a virtual product is affiliated with a real-world source? To make things even more complicated, AR provides an environment that mixes the real world and the trademarks presented therein with a virtual world that may augment and distort the real world. Thus, trademark owners may face difficulties when asserting trademark infringement claims against allegedly infringing uses in the AR/VR context.

A trademark owner may not be able to prove that there is a likelihood of confusion as to the source or affiliation of the virtual product. In practice, a developer or operator of an AR/VR experience may expressly deny affiliation with the trademark owner, may merely be offering a critique of the trademark, or may find a defense to infringement claiming nominative fair use. Nominative fair use provides that the use of a mark is not infringing if such use is descriptive of and is used fairly and in good faith only to describe the goods or services of the trademark owner. This analysis of confusion of the end user or consumer turns on the manner in which the virtual marks are being presented to the end user. Is the AR/VR experience a form of entertainment, where the use of marks is irreverent or embodies some parody or commentary on the real-world trademark? If so, a reasonable end user may not think the mark owner was the source, and the trademark owner may not be able to establish that there was indeed a likelihood of confusion in the virtual use.

What is the result when AR content is displayed after recognizing real-world trademarks? Consider for a moment an AR experience that provides historical information or commentary as an overlay when a real-world trademark is within view of the end user. In this instance, the real-world trademark is intended to convey the goodwill that the trademark has built up in the mark. But the trademark owner may not have any editorial control over the virtual commentary and may instead find that such commentary is diluting the goodwill and distinctive quality of the real-world mark.

When a library is a creator of content, consideration should be given to the intent and means of the presentation of real-world trademarks in the virtual content. Having AR content triggered from recognizable, real-world trademarks may only invite challenges from the trademark owner. After all, trademark owners are required to police their mark.

When a library is a curator of content or an operator of an AR/VR experience, where the content is created by other parties, the library should consider requiring that developers or content creators make warranties and representations that they own the content and that the content does not infringe the rights of others. Again, the offering of an AR/VR service as part of the library system will turn on the express provisions in the agreements between the necessary parties.

PATENTS

Patents allow an inventor to prevent others from making, using, or selling a claimed invention in a given jurisdiction.[15] In the AR/VR context, patent claims have been granted to cover the hardware used to provide the AR/VR experience, interfaces that deliver the content to the end user, and even methods relating to processing content and presenting content in an AR/VR experience. Universities, corporations, and individuals are filing patent applications in the AR/VR sector on a regular basis. These patent applications are often not published for at least eighteen months after filing. Yet, once they are granted, those that are using the claimed invention in a manner proscribed by the granted patent claims are exposed to a patent infringement action.

As an example, on January 30, 2018, Barbaro Technologies sued Niantic for the alleged infringement of U.S. Patent Nos. 7,373,377 and 8,228,325. The asserted patent claims are related to integrating real-time information into a virtual thematic environment using a computer system. Barbaro specifically asserts that both Niantic's Pokémon GO and Ingress infringe the asserted patent claims. Similarly, the battle between patented AR/VR hardware and control software is not showing signs of slowing, since Microsoft was sued by Holotouch for allegedly infringing claims directed to a holographic human-machine interface.

Of particular interest are entities such as Lennon Image Technologies that have enforced their patent rights by targeting multiple defendants in a campaign of patent litigations. The Lennon Image Technologies patents relate generally to a method of capturing a customer's image "at a retailer's place of business" and blending it with prerecorded "models wearing apparel items" in order to allow the customer "to virtually assess the selected merchandise without actually having to try on the apparel."

We discussed in this chapter the number of different parties that may be involved in providing an AR/VR experience. As libraries prepare to take on an offering such as an AR/VR service, it may become evident that the resources are not available to consider all of the potential liabilities under the multiple of granted patent claims in this space. As with the retail industry and the virtual modeling, a patent law suit alleging infringement of claims for providing certain AR/VR services could have an irreversible and chilling impact on the library's ability to maintain its AR/VR services. Therefore, it is imperative to contractually insulate the library from the risks and liabilities that may be inherent in adopting an AR/VR service. Of course, if a library were to endeavor to develop its own proprietary AR/VR service offering, consideration should be given to understanding the patent landscape in this area and the freedoms to operate a particular AR/VR service.

PRIVACY AND DATA

We live in a world of data. But legislation that governs how entities collect, use, and manage user data is not consistent across jurisdictions. This is most notably evidenced by the recent implementation of the General Data Protection Regulation, which governs data protections for data relating to citizens of the European Union. Libraries across the United States are frequented by domestic patrons and foreign patrons alike. Thus, as laws are enacted that govern not only actions within the borders of a given jurisdiction, but the personal data of citizens of foreign jurisdictions, the burden on domestic entities such as libraries is ever increasing. Moreover, when a library decides to offer an AR/VR service that potentially includes collection of end-user data, storage of data, and use of the data to provide an AR/VR experience, it should be aware of the laws and regulations governing such data.

For example, certain AR/VR platforms may track a user's location, head movement, eye movement, and other user preferences in order to provide the AR/VR experience. As the technology advances, additional end-user metrics may be collected to improve the AR/VR experience. Therefore, it is important to understand what information is being collected, where this information is going to be stored, and how the information is being used. At each transfer and storage of this data, privacy concerns abound. Such privacy risks mean that the developers and operators of the AR/VR experience must have clarity on at least the collection, storage, and use of end-user data. Privacy policies defining what is being collected and how such data may be used should be clear, and privacy notices should be provided to end users in accordance with all applicable laws and regulations.

Moreover, when data is being controlled by an entity such as a library, the security of such data must also be considered. Data breaches have sadly become regular occurrences among domestic entities, and the library must take steps to provide appropriate security measures over such data or to contract how such data will be stored, if at all.

CONCLUSION

Libraries and librarians have a vested interest in the development and enforcement of the laws governing intellectual property rights. Libraries continue to play a role as archives of information and as forums for accessing data, whether it be printed or virtual. As libraries evolve to advance their critical role in promoting the arts and sciences, and the history of the same, new risks become evident. In the challenging and changing world of the library sciences, unmitigated risks may hinder the worthy goal of adopting emerging technology as a mechanism to reach a broader cross-section of the public. But with careful consideration, guidance from legal counsel, and a thoroughly defined set of terms and agreements, libraries may indeed be the most suitable forum to embrace the limitless possibilities of AR/VR in the information age.

NOTES

1. It should be noted that the following is for educational purposes and is not to be considered legal advice. The complexities of the following legal principles applied to an emerging technology such as AR/VR have created many unanswered questions in the legal community. Many legal scholars expect many of these issues to be clarified in legislation or through the courts over the next several years.

2. 17 U.S.C. § 102.

3. *Feist Publications, Inc. v. Rural Tel. Serv. Co.*, 499 U.S. 340, 361 (1991).

4. Melville B. Nimmer and David Nimmer, *Nimmer on Copyright* § 13.01[A] (2011).

5. See Nimmer and Nimmer; see also *U.S. Department of Justice Criminal Resources Manual 1854.*

6. See 17 U.S.C. § 109(d).

7. See *U.S. Department of Justice Criminal Resources Manual 1854.*

8. There has been wide debate over companies that sell equipment but try to maintain control over the software that makes the equipment work.

9. 17 U.S.C. § 512(k).

10. See 17 U.S.C. § 107.

11. See 17 U.S.C. § 107.

12. 15 U.S.C. § 1127.

13. 15 U.S.C. §§ 1114, 1125.

14. *Polaroid Corp. v. Polarad Elect. Corp.*, 287 F.2d 492 (2d Cir.), cert. denied, 368 U.S. 820 (1961).

15. See 35 U.S.C. 271.

About the Contributors

BRIGITTE BELL joined the University of St. Francis Library staff in 2012 as an instruction librarian. She currently serves as the library's reference and instruction manager. Bell received her BA in English from Dominican University in 2010 and her MLIS degree in 2012. She began her career at the Dominican University Library, where she worked from 2007 to 2010. In additional to library instructional materials delivery and development, Bell instructs in the University of St. Francis's freshman first-year experience program and its business school. She is currently working on a master of business administration degree.

TALLIE CASUCCI is an assistant librarian at the University of Utah's J. Willard Marriott Library. Currently, she is the liaison to the departments of Bioengineering, Entertainment Arts & Engineering, and Health, Kinesiology & Recreation. Additionally, she works with the Marriott Library's team on patent support. Casucci helps faculty, staff, and students discover evidence-based knowledge and research, patents and existing technologies, competitive intelligence, and potential partners and resources for the creation of new inventions. Previously, Casucci worked at the Spencer S. Eccles Health Sciences Library as the innovation librarian. She graduated from the University of North Carolina at Chapel Hill with a BA degree in exercise and sport science. Afterwards, she completed an MLIS at the University of Pittsburgh with a specialization in health resources and services.

CHAD CLARK received his master's degree from the Dominican School of Library and Information Studies in 2011. He currently serves as the assistant director at the Highland Park Public Library in Highland Park, Illinois. He is committed to empowering people outside the technology industry to participate meaningfully in a networked world. Clark has presented at numerous conferences, including Creative Libraries Utah and Colorado and the Public Library Association. Most recently he authored a chapter about hackerspaces in *The Makerspace Librarian's Sourcebook* (2017).

MATT COOK is head of emerging technologies for the University of Oklahoma Libraries. In his role as an educational technologist, he has cofounded two university makerspaces, earned *Campus Technology* "Innovator" and "Education Futurist" awards, and been named a *Library Journal* "Mover & Shaker." Cook has developed and deployed a beacon-based indoor navigation app (OU Libraries' NavApp), interactive mindfulness technology (Sparq Labyrinth), and a custom-designed virtual reality workstation (OVAL) that is currently being used by more than a dozen academic disciplines. His research primarily concerns spatial cognition and scholarly technology, and he has presented on related topics in the United States and abroad.

TERRY COTTRELL is vice president for operations and technology and CIO at the University of St. Francis in Joliet, Illinois. Cottrell's recent publications and presentations cover e-science research trends, the effects of media on learning, hands-free augmented reality tools, copyright, instructional technology history, IT leadership and finance, mobile device management, and other topics. He holds EdD, MS, and MBA degrees and CEH certification. He currently teaches research methods, technology trends, and writing at the University of St. Francis. He has taught and designed various management and business classes at Colorado State University-Global Campus, and at Computers for Educators at Northern Illinois University. He is currently designing and teaching CIS 453: Advanced Cybersecurity at Northwestern University.

THOMAS FERRILL, who goes by the nickname T.J., is an assistant head of Creativity & Innovation Services in the J. Willard Marriott Library at the University of Utah, and he heads up the Marriott Library's Creative Spaces, which includes interactive media such as augmented and virtual reality, 3D printing, and 3D scanning. One of T.J.'s main goals is to remove and reduce the barriers to entry for library patrons who wish to incorporate new technology elements in their scholarship. In addition to building and configuring these services, T.J. is also involved in projects that leverage these technologies to help students, educators, and researchers reach their goals. This includes collaborations focused on virtual reality learning environments, data visualization projects using 3D printers, the replication of rare and special collections, and a constant stream of 3D printing projects. T.J. has a master's degree in public administration from the University of Utah, and he studied philosophy and computer science as an undergraduate.

GREG HATCH is a librarian at the University of Utah's J. Willard Marriott Library, where he is the head of Creativity & Innovation, and the liaison to theatre, dance, and film and media arts. His department offers collaborative support and expertise to scholars in their trans-disciplinary research and productivity, with an emphasis on arts and design, media production, multimodal communication, fabrication technology, and interactive media. Hatch's scholarly and creative research interests meet at the intersection of information science and the arts, exploring visual literacy and communication, data visualization, and interdisciplinary applications of the arts. He earned an MLIS degree at the University of Washington and a BA in theatre at Saint John's University, Minnesota.

R. BRUCE JENSEN, another University of Washington graduate (BA, English), helms the STEAMworks makerspace in the library at Kutztown University of Pennsylvania. With Jesse Warner, he cofounded its Zine Library which extends the DIY/DIT maker ethic to print publishing. As emerging technologies librarian, he is liaison to the Anthropology, Modern Languages, and Cinema, Television and Media Production departments. He worked with *Críticas* magazine throughout its history where he team-blogged with Loida Garcia-Febo on *Multicultural Link*. He has handled thousands of IRC reference transactions since 2001 with the service that is now OCLC's QuestionPoint. With graduate degrees from UCLA (library science) and Northern Arizona University (language teaching), plus undergraduate studies in computer science and languages, Jensen still has a lot to learn.

BOHYUN KIM is the chief technology officer and an associate professor at the University of Rhode Island Libraries. She is the author of two books—*Understanding Gamification* (2015) and *Library Mobile Experience: Practices and User Expectations* (2013)—and the founding editor of the Association of College & Research Libraries' *TechConnect* blog. She is currently the president of the Library and Information Technology Association (LITA) and serves on the advisory boards and committees of the ALA Office for Information Technology Policy and San Jose State University School of Information.

ZACK LISCHER-KATZ is a postdoctoral research fellow in data curation at the University of Oklahoma Libraries. In his fellowship, he is developing guidelines for curating research data associated with virtual reality technologies and 3D models, and he is studying the impact of virtual reality and 3D tools on research and pedagogy in academic libraries. His personal research looks at techniques for preserving visual forms of information and practices of visual knowledge production in the context of archives, libraries, and museums. He received his PhD in communication, information, and library studies from Rutgers University's School of Communication and Information.

AUSTIN OLNEY is a digital media specialist at the White Plains Public Library (New York). He teaches patrons to be digitally literate and provides them with the technology skills necessary for the modern world. Using the library's teen space as a backdrop, he presents students with a hands-on approach. He received his MS degree in education from SUNY Cortland in 2011. He has experience teaching in a variety of educational institutions, and enjoys applying advanced technology skills to actively engage students with diverse backgrounds and learning styles.

BRANDON PATTERSON is the technology engagement librarian at the Eccles Health Sciences Library at the University of Utah. He connects students, staff, and faculty to digital tools and emerging technologies and creates meaningful experiences using prototyping tools, virtual reality, and online learning platforms. Patterson's scholarly interests include space-making and engaged learning centered in and around libraries. He is currently working on projects that involve the creation of scholarly technology spaces, the information literacy of professional nurses, and collaborative makerspace projects in the health sciences. Patterson earned an MS degree in information and an MA degree in higher education from the University of Michigan, and he studied communication and international studies as an undergraduate at the University of Utah.

MICHAEL RIESEN is an intellectual property attorney and partner with the firm Baker&Hostetler, LLP. He manages patent and trademark portfolios, and provides enforcement strategies to leverage the portfolios in offensive and defensive manners. Riesen uses his technical background in material sciences, physics, electrical engineering, and computer science to assist in intellectual property due diligence and patent litigation, and he works with clients to quickly assess their cases and develop effective strategies. A former high school and college physics teacher, he capitalizes on his ability to understand complex and high-level scientific concepts and to effectively convey these concepts to inventors, counsel, judges, juries, and examiners. Academically, Riesen has been published for his research in machine learning and artificial intelligence. Currently, he works with pioneers in AR/VR and mixed reality technologies to protect and monetize inventions in this sector.

FELICIA A. SMITH is the head of learning and outreach at the Stanford University Libraries. She supervises reference, outreach, and instructional services. She published a book titled *Cybrarian Extraordinaire: Compelling Information Literacy Instruction* (2011), and several scholarly articles detailing her educational games with learning objectives. Her article "Games for Teaching

Information Literacy Skills" has been downloaded over 7,000 times in over 100 countries. Her publications illustrate her successful active learning exercises and explain why she once taught class dressed in a full pirate costume. Smith taught popular classes in the Virtual World of Second Life. She created an information literacy program using Kindle e-readers for inmates in a Juvenile Justice Center. She is experimenting with flipped classroom concepts to allow more class time for critical thinking and search strategy instruction. Previously, Smith worked as a criminal defense private investigator in Chicago, specializing in homicide and narcotics, and she was required to carry a .357 Magnum pistol.

Index